WEST SUSSEX PUB WALKS

David Weller

COUNTRYSIDE BOOKS
NEWBURY BERKSHIRE

First published 2019
© 2019 David Weller
Revised and reprinted 2023

All rights reserved. No part of this publication may be reproduced, stored in a retrieval system, or transmitted by any means, electronic, mechanical, photocopying, recording or otherwise, without the prior written permission of the copyright holder and publishers.

COUNTRYSIDE BOOKS
3 Catherine Road
Newbury, Berkshire

To view our complete range of books,
please visit us at
www.countrysidebooks.co.uk

ISBN 978 1 84674 387 0

All materials used in the manufacture of this book carry FSC certification

Designed by KT Designs, St Helens

Produced through The Letterworks Ltd., Reading
Typeset by KT Designs, St Helens
Printed by Holywell Press, Oxford

CONTENTS

Area map 5
Introduction 6

WALK

1 Stoughton: The Hare & Hounds (4 miles/6.4km) 7
2 West Itchenor: The Ship Inn (7¼ miles/11.6km) 11
3 Milland: The Rising Sun (3½ miles/5.6km) 16
4 Chilgrove: The White Horse (4¼ miles/6.8km) 21
5 Sidlesham Quay: The Crab & Lobster (3½ miles/5.6km) 26
6 Halfway Bridge: The Halfway Bridge Inn (6 miles/9.6km) 30
7 Heyshott: The Unicorn Inn (4¼ miles/6.8km) 34
8 Lurgashall: The Noah's Ark (3½ miles/5.6km) 38
9 Burpham: The George at Burpham (4½ miles/7.2km) 42
10 Amberley: The Bridge Inn (6 miles/9.6km) 46
11 Loxwood: The Onslow Arms (5½ miles/8.8km) 51
12 Billingshurst: The Limeburners (3¼ miles/5.2km) 56
13 Rudgwick: The Kings Head (3 miles/4.8km) 60
14 Findon: The Village House (4 miles/6.4km) 64

15 Bramber: The Castle Inn Hotel (2½ miles/4km)   68
16 Rusper: The Plough & Attic Rooms
    (4½ miles/7.2km)   73
17 Nuthurst: The Black Horse Inn (3½ miles/5.6km)   78
18 Henfield: The Old Railway (4¼ miles/6.8km)   82
19 Pyecombe: The Plough (6½ miles/10.4km)   86
20 Balcombe: The Half Moon Inn (7¼ miles/11.6km)   91

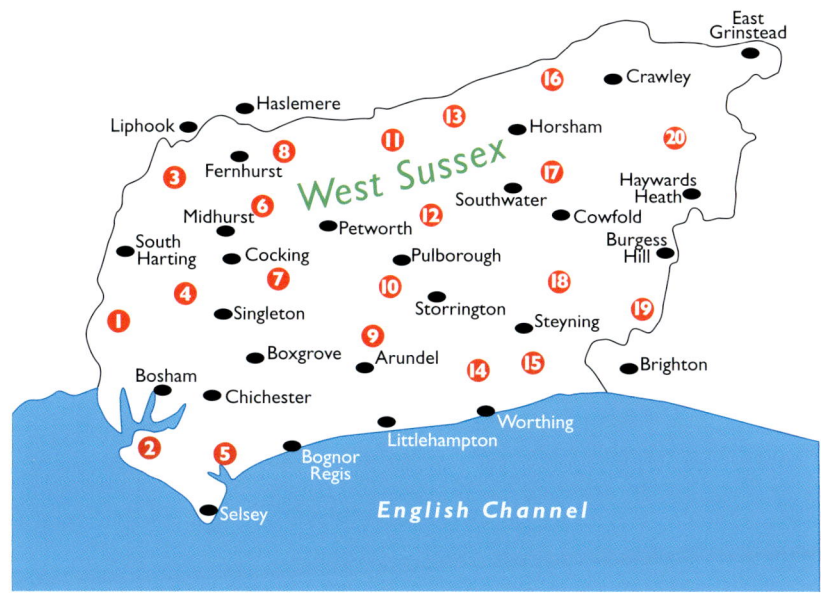

PUBLISHER'S NOTE

We hope that you obtain considerable enjoyment from this book; great care has been taken in its preparation. Although at the time of publication all routes followed public rights of way or permitted paths, diversion orders can be made and permissions withdrawn.

We cannot, of course, be held responsible for such diversion orders and any inaccuracies in the text which result from these or any other changes to the routes, nor any damage which might result from walkers trespassing on private property. We are anxious though that all the details covering the walks are kept up to date and would therefore welcome information from readers which would be relevant to future editions.

The simple sketch maps that accompany the walks in this book are based on notes made by the author whilst checking out the routes on the ground. They are designed to show you how to reach the start, to point out the main features of the overall circuit and they contain a progression of numbers that relate to the paragraphs of the text.

However, for the benefit of a proper map, we do recommend that you purchase the relevant Ordnance Survey sheet covering your walk. The Ordnance Survey maps are widely available, especially through booksellers and local newsagents.

INTRODUCTION

West Sussex is a wonderfully diverse county and such a joy to explore on foot. To the south-west are the shimmering waters of Chichester Harbour where pretty sailboats bob at their moorings while just along the coast are the golden sands of West Wittering beach that is popular with holidaymakers and day-trippers. Nearby are the isolated tidal saltmarsh lagoons of Pagham Harbour Nature Reserve that is teeming with bird life.

Further inland, the ground rises to the heights of the rolling downs in the newly created South Downs National Park and it is here that the hilltops offer far-reaching views while below lie quiet wooded valleys that are alive with birdsong. Added to this panorama are the meandering waters of the Arun, Adur, Ouse and Wey rivers plus the streams that feed them as they make their way slowly to the sea. These waterways are a lifeline to the wildlife they support while their banks are lined with rushes and wild flowers.

All these wonderful scenes are visited during the walks I have devised and, to top it all, dotted around the county are pretty towns, villages and hamlets where welcoming pubs are situated – some many centuries old. It is from these pubs that the 20 circular walks here are based and I have also suggested interesting places you may wish to visit nearby. Although I have made some mention of the drinks and food on offer, these were at the time of writing and of course they may well have changed since then.

So, whether it's a hot summer's day when you seek shade under an umbrella at a table in a rose-bowered pub garden overlooking the countryside, or maybe during winter when you wish to snuggle up to a log fire burning in the grate of the cosy bar, there will always be a cheery welcome and a hearty meal to enjoy.

While these instructions and sketch maps will get you around the circuits easily, I always recommend you take the appropriate OS map that will give a better overview of the route. Another recommendation I always make is to wear good walking boots or shoes that offer support on uneven or slippery ground.

Cheers to happy walking!

David Weller

Walk 1
STOUGHTON

Distance: 4 miles (6.4 km)

Map: OS Explorer OL8 Chichester, South Harting & Selsey
Grid Ref: SU803115

How to get there: Stoughton is 5½ miles north-west of Chichester. From the B2141, half a mile west of Chilgrove, go west on a lane signed to East Marden. Fork left through the village to reach Stoughton and The Hare & Hounds in 2½ miles. **Sat Nav:** PO18 9JQ.

Parking: At the Hare & Hounds, with permission, or considerately nearby beside the village street.

Pretty Stoughton village is strung out along the floor of an unspoilt valley with the slopes of Inholmes Wood to its north and Kingley Vale to the east. This easy-to-follow route offers superb panoramic views as it soon leaves the village street by following

West Sussex Pub Walks

the Monarch's Way long-distance path to the top of Stoughton Down. The not-too-difficult climb brings you to magnificent woodland on its crest where the route turns south and passes by Bow Hill. Here the way continues along an ancient trackway that passes a group of well preserved Bronze Age bell barrows with distant views to the sea. Turning once again, the route heads back to the village below via a wonderful track that offers spectacular panoramic views over the valley and the surrounding countryside towards Chichester.

THE PUB

THE HARE & HOUNDS has been the focal point of the village since the 19th century and while the interior, food and beers have changed since that time, the timeless quality of its setting certainly has not. This privately owned free house takes pride in its well-kept bitters, lagers and ciders; many of which are award winners. The pub is open all day and offers a good range of home-cooked food; from simple lunchtime baguettes through soup of the day to a selection of more substantial meals. On a summer's day why not put your feet up after the walk and relax at a table under a colourful umbrella in the sunny front garden and soak up the peace and tranquility the valley offers?
⊕ hareandhoundspub.co.uk ☎ 02392 631433

Stoughton 1

The Walk

1 With your back to the pub, go left along the village street to soon meet a concrete drive on your right by a house called **Old Bartons**. Turn right along the drive, pass by a barn and fork left on the signed **Monarch's Way** long-distance path.

2 Press on along the rising track that becomes steeper as it nears the top of **Stoughton Down** and meets a junction of tracks by a directional post. Turn right on a wide track signed as a bridleway. Very soon fork left by a direction post as the bridleway narrows and rises through woodland. As you near the top of the incline, look out for a directional post on your right.

3 Turn right here on a narrow downhill bridleway that soon rejoins the wide track left earlier. Turn left along the track that later passes an open area marked on maps as the **Devil's Humps**. The view seaward here is stunning.

The Devil's Humps are Bronze Age bell barrows which are listed Scheduled Ancient Monuments. The large number of cross dykes

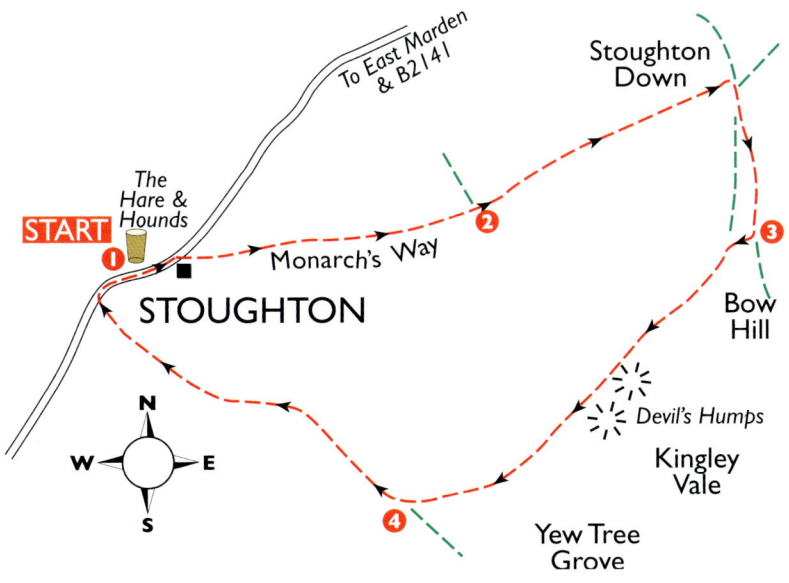

West Sussex Pub Walks

(prehistoric land boundaries) and tumuli (burial mounds) in this area indicates that these hills were populated by early man.

Press on along the track that becomes grassed over and continues through woodland before ending at a T-junction with a field ahead of you.

4 Turn right and follow a downhill track that later passes between fields. Look out for a poignant memorial on your right to a brave young man who gave his life for our freedom.

The memorial is to a 23-year-old Polish flying ace, pilot officer Bolesław Własnowolski V.M. K.W. He was killed when his Hurricane was shot down by a Messerschmitt 109 and crashed into this field on 1 November 1940. He is buried in Chichester.

The track ends at the village street where a right turn brings you back to **The Hare & Hounds** to complete this good circuit.

Place of Interest Nearby

Uppark House and Garden is a National Trust gem sitting on top of the South Downs surrounded by its restored 19th-century gardens. The Georgian interior illustrates the comfortable lives of those who lived 'upstairs' while displaying the contrast of the servants' quarters 'below stairs'. The house is 5 miles north of Stoughton off the B2146 at South Harting, Petersfield. **Sat Nav:** GU31 5QR. Check for opening times.
🌐 nationaltrust.org.uk/uppark-house-and-garden
☎ 01730 825415

West Wittering village

Walk 2
West Itchenor

Distance: 7¼ miles (11.6 km)

Map: OS Explorer OL8 Chichester, South Harting & Selsey
Grid Ref: SU799013

How to get there: West Itchenor is south-west of Chichester. From the A27 bypass, follow the A286 south and at a roundabout go ahead on the B2179 before forking right on the signed Itchenor road. **Sat Nav:** PO20 7AH.

Parking: At The Ship Inn, with permission, or in the signed pay and display car park 50 yards before meeting the pub.

The picturesque sailing village of West Itchenor sits on the eastern shores of Chichester Harbour which is designated as an Area of Wetland of International Importance as well as being an Area of Outstanding Natural Beauty; just two of its accolades. The area has much to offer, not just for the sailors who anchor

West Sussex Pub Walks

here but also for walkers and birdwatchers. It is home to the Chichester Harbour Conservancy that oversees the harbour as a nature reserve where sailors, walkers and wildlife co-exist peacefully. After leaving the pub, the route soon crosses level fields to meet West Wittering where a road leads you through the village to meet the coast. The way then turns and continues along a mile of golden sands before meeting and following the water's edge of the Chichester Channel.

THE PUB **THE SHIP INN** is in the heart of the village and being only 200 yards from the water's edge is popular with sailors mooring here and walkers enjoying the New Lipchis Way long-distance path that passes close by. The pub is open all day and offers a good selection of locally sourced fresh food from a choice of sandwiches and ploughman's to lovely home-cooked staples such as sausage and creamy mash or a delicious fish pie. It goes without saying that there is also a good selection of beers, spirits and wines to suit all tastes. The Ship Inn is very popular at weekends and it is best to book a table if you wish to eat here in the evening.
🌐 theshipinnitchenor.co.uk ☎ 01243 512284

The Walk

❶ From the pub, walk back along the village street, passing interesting individually designed houses. At a sharp left bend in the road turn right, pass the entrance drive to **Itchenor Park Farmhouse** and follow a well-trodden path signed as the **Salterns Way** to the rear of the village **Memorial Hall**.

The Salterns Way is a 12-mile (19km) cycle route from the centre of Chichester to the beach at West Wittering.

❷ The path soon meets and continues alongside arable fields. Keep to the path after crossing a concrete farm drive until it eventually meets a T-junction with a wide track known as **Sheepwash Lane**.

❸ Turn right and continue along **Sheepwash Lane** until it meets with a road. Cross the road to the pavement opposite and turn right. Now follow this pavement into **West Wittering** village.

West Itchenor 2

Pass the **Memorial Hall** and later, **The Old House At Home** pub. Ignore side roads.

4. As you begin to leave the village behind, look out for **Berrybarn Lane** on your right. Turn right along this private road that is also

West Sussex Pub Walks

a public bridleway and, at its end, pass a gate and go ahead to meet the golden sands of **West Wittering beach**, that must be a contender for the best in southern England.

❺ Turn right and walk along the beach for about a mile. Soon after passing the last of the beach huts, look out for a tall beacon and 50 metres later climb the shingle bank to enter a car park.

❻ Go ahead over a turning area and continue between posts to meet a well-trodden path between trees. This path is the **New Lipchis Way** long-distance path that after 3 miles brings you back to **West Itchenor**.

The New Lipchis Way long-distance path is 39 miles long, beginning in Liphook, Hampshire and ending here at the mouth of Chichester Harbour. The name is an amalgam of the two town names.

❼ Keep ahead on the path when you meet an area of grassland with houses to your right.

West Itchenor

8 Pass through a gate and continue through a second on your immediate left.

9 Follow the path between gardens to meet a short drive with a kissing gate at its end. Press on along the path ignoring the occasional side path to eventually pass through a boatyard to rejoin the village street with **The Ship Inn** to your right.

Place of Interest Nearby

Fishbourne Roman Palace & Gardens is 1 mile west of Chichester off the A259 in the village of Fishbourne. The site displays the largest and most spectacular collection of in-situ floor mosaics in Britain. Also recreated here are what are thought to be the earliest Roman gardens in the country. **Sat Nav:** PO19 3QR.
🌐 sussexpast.co.uk/properties-to-discover/fishbourne-roman-palace
☎ 01243 785859

West Wittering beach

Walk 3
MILLAND

Distance: 3½ miles (5.6 km)

Map: OS Explorer OL33 Haslemere & Petersfield
Grid Ref: SU838269

How to get there: Milland is 4 miles west of the A286 at Fernhurst. From the crossroads in the centre of Fernhurst, go west along Vann Road and follow the signs to meet Milland and the crossroads by The Rising Sun pub. **Sat Nav:** GU30 7NA.

Parking: At The Rising Sun, with permission, or by the roadside nearby.

Milland ③

Milland is an attractive village sitting astride the old Roman Chichester to Silchester Road and tucked up against the Hampshire border not far from Liphook. The village still retains its village green and of course a pub, the welcoming Rising Sun. The walk leaves the village by following a small section of the Roman road before continuing along the pristine drive to Lyford Farm and across a couple of its fields. Joining a quiet, little-used lane, the route meets the strangely named hamlet of Titty Hill and an ancient byway. Turning back towards Milland the byway leads through peaceful woodland where the quiet walker has a good chance of spotting a deer or two. After meeting a farm lane the way soon crosses level fields to rejoin the village.

THE PUB **THE RISING SUN** sits in a prominent position at the village crossroads and opposite the green. The popular pub serves well-kept beers such as London Pride, Chiswick and HSB plus a good selection of food using local produce. All the favourites are here; fish and chips, juicy steaks, veggie dishes, summer salads and look out for the chef's specials board. Better still, why not enjoy lunch at a table in the shade of a colourful parasol in the lovely garden or on the terrace during summer and relax awhile after your walk? Watch out for the traditional pub hours of Monday to Thursday 12noon until 3pm and 5.30pm to 12midnight. Fridays, and weekends the pub is open from 12noon until midnight.
⊕ risingsunmilland.com ☎ 01428 741347

The Walk

❶ With your back to the pub, go left along the road to pass **Milland Stores and Café**. Press on along the quiet road that traces the old Roman road and pass **Waldergrove Farm** and later **Milland Evangelical Chapel** to reach a right bend and the drive to **Lyford Farm** on your left.

❷ Turn left and continue along the drive to **Lyford Farm**.

The remains of a Roman posting station have been found in the field to your right here. These stations were relay points that provided fresh horses for dispatch riders and generally housed not much more than a smithy.

West Sussex Pub Walks

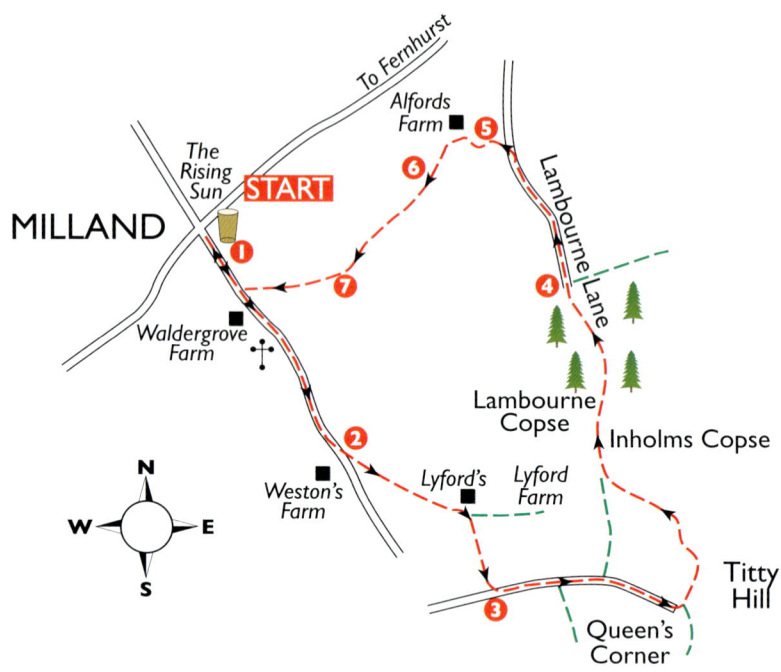

When opposite a house named **Lyford's**, turn right over a stile and go ahead along a field edge. Pass a field byre and continue ahead alongside the next field to reach a country lane.

❸ Turn left along this little-used lane until it ends in the hamlet of **Titty Hill**. Go ahead to a directional post and turn left along a signed restricted byway that enters woodland. Keep to the sometimes narrow byway through this lovely woodland and ignore a couple of crossing forestry tracks.

❹ At the end of woodland, continue ahead along a drive for just under ½ a mile and look out for railings on either side where it crosses a brook. Here, cross a hidden stile on your left. *If you meet the drive to **Alfords Farm** you have gone too far.* After crossing the stile, turn right alongside the hedgerow to reach a ranch-style fence beside the drive to **Alfords Farm**. Turn left beside the fence and cross a further style at the end of the paddock.

Milland 3

5 Follow the signed path by forking right along the drive and fork right again in 50 metres by a gate. Now follow a fenced path to meet a gate at a field edge and a fingerpost. Go left on a shingle drive before forking right by a barn to meet a gate. Ignore a path signed on your left and press on ahead over a field to a second gate.

6 Enter a field and press on to its far corner and pass through a kissing gate. Cross a stile ahead of you and continue along the right side of the next field. Cross a stile at its end and go through the centre of the next field to a stile in the hedgerow opposite. Cross this and a second to pass by the side of a house and another stile.

7 Now go ahead and slightly right to the far corner to meet the road walked earlier. Turn right along the road to meet **The Rising Sun** pub and the end of this good circuit.

West Sussex Pub Walks

Place of Interest Nearby

Milland Pottery is just ½ mile north of the Rising Sun pub in Milland Lane. Tucked away down a track beside Milland Farmhouse, the pottery has a small showroom displaying pots from the potter's wheel. The pottery is run by ceramicist Angela Carter who welcomes commissions for special occasions such as weddings and birthdays. Open most weekdays and Saturday mornings (not Sundays or Mondays) it is best to telephone first before visiting. **Sat Nav:** GU30 7JP.
⊕ millandpottery.co.uk ☎ 01428 741530.

Walk 4
CHILGROVE

Distance: 4¼ miles (6.8 km))
Map: OS Explorer OL8 Chichester & Selsey **Grid Ref:** SU827144
How to get there: Chilgrove is 7 miles north-west of Chichester. Go north on the A286 from Chichester, pass East Lavant and turn left on the B2141 to reach Chilgrove and The White Horse in 3½ miles. **Sat Nav:** PO18 9HX.
Parking: At The White Horse, with permission, or nearby.

Chilgrove is no more than a hamlet and much of that is hidden from those travelling the B2141 road that passes the prominent White Horse pub. The walk begins by crossing fields to join with a cart track that leads through magnificent woodland to meet up with Hooksway where the isolated Royal Oak pub and its sunny garden are passed. From here the way follows a byway that gains height and momentarily meets the South Downs

West Sussex Pub Walks

Way at **Philliswood Down**. The route then begins its return to Chilgrove through open fields with expansive views and passes by the lost village of Monkton, now no more than a depression in the grasses. The way then continues along a lovely track and later a quiet lane that ends back at The White Horse.

THE PUB **THE WHITE HORSE** is a lovely pub that has won an AA rosette for 'Best Pub' in 2015 as well as winning GQ magazine's Food & Drink awards for the chefs who cook with ingredients that are locally produced from the surrounding area such as venison from nearby estates or the Goodwood cheeses that are a regular feature. The pub offers a choice of fine dining from a constantly changing menu in the restaurant and a choice of snacks in the bar area. On a sunny day why not enjoy the scrumptious food with a glass or two in the superbly kept side garden where tables with sun umbrellas provide the perfect relaxing setting? Children are welcome and dogs are well provided for with water bowls.
🌐 thewhitehorse.co.uk   ☎ 01243 519444

Chilgrove 4

The Walk

1 From the pub, walk back to the B2141 and turn right along the grass verge. In 55 metres, fork right through a kissing gate and go ahead on a grassy path. Pass through a second kissing gate and cross a field. Cross a farm drive and press on ahead along the right side of the next field. Pass through a line of trees and continue ahead to meet a track signed as a bridleway.

2 Turn right along the track and at gates fork left on the bridleway that continues through the peace and tranquillity of **Phillis Wood**. After 1 mile, the bridleway ends opposite **The Royal Oak** pub in **Hooksway**.

West Sussex Pub Walks

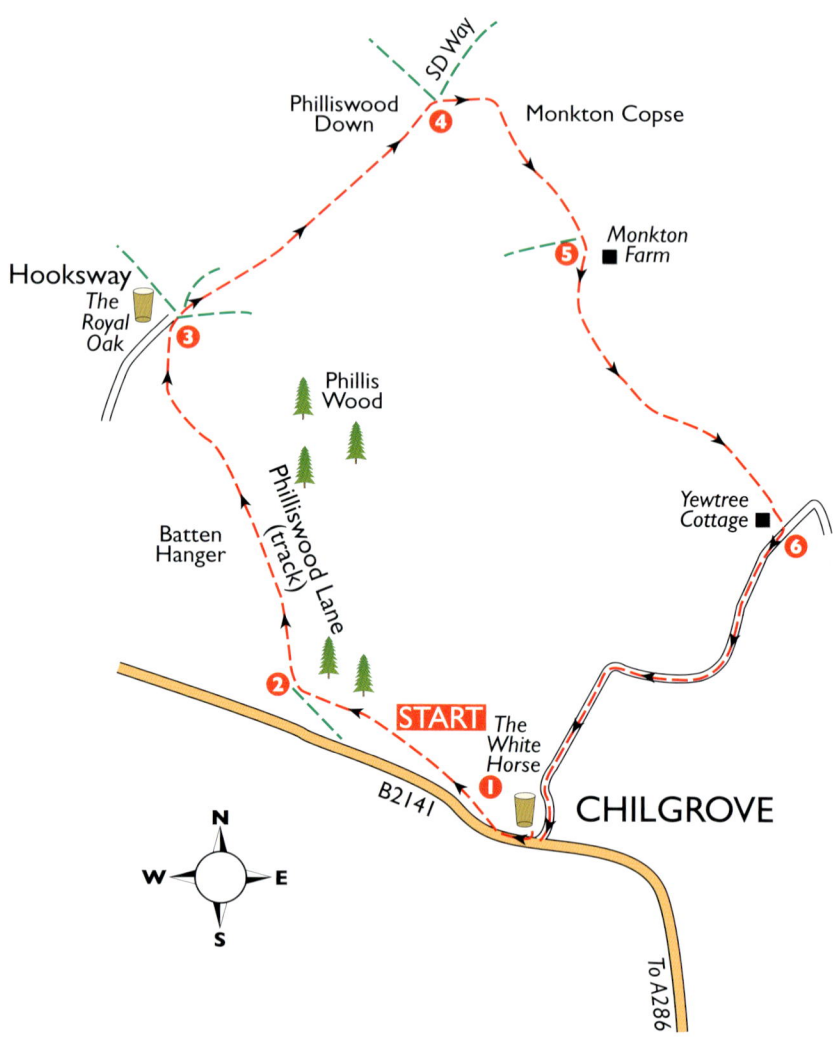

The 16th-century Royal Oak is the only building in Hooksway to have survived after the villagers were wiped out by bubonic plague.

③ Turn right here on a track. Ignore a footpath by the pub car park and go ahead on the stony track that soon divides. Fork right and

Chilgrove ④

continue on the signed byway that begins to climb up **Philliswood Down**. Later ignore a right fork and press on uphill to meet a junction of tracks and the signed **South Downs Way**.

④ Turn right on a signed footpath, enter a field and continue ahead along its edge to meet a directional post. Turn right; go down the slope and cross a stile beside a gate before continuing alongside power cables down this lovely grassy valley.

On the left are the indistinct remains of the medieval village of Monkton, now little more than a depression in the grasses. By 1608, only the farmhouse remained which was finally demolished a century ago. Unlike Hooksway, it is believed the 16th-century Enclosure Act caused the demise of the hamlet when its inhabitants lost their livelihoods.

⑤ Cross a stile by a second gate and continue ahead. When opposite a flint barn, fork slightly right on a cart track to meet and pass through a gate. Continue on a track that eventually ends at a little-used country lane.

⑥ Turn right along the lane that in 1 mile brings you back to **The White Horse** and the end of this good walk.

Place of Interest Nearby

West Dean Gardens are said to be one of the greatest restored gardens open to the public today. There is an Edwardian pergola, Victorian glasshouses and a restored walled kitchen garden plus a wide range of features to explore. There is also a gift shop and restaurant. Open from February to December from 10.30am to 5pm weekdays and 9am to 5pm at weekends. The gardens are off the A286, 5 miles east of Chilgrove. **Sat Nav:** PO18 0RX.
🌐 westdean.org.uk/gardens   ☎ 01243 818210

Walk 5
SIDLESHAM QUAY

Distance: 3½ miles (5.6 km)

Map: OS Explorer OL8 Chichester, South Harting & Selsey
Grid Ref: SZ861972

How to get there: From the A27 south of Chichester go south on the B2145 signed to Selsey. Once in Sidlesham and just after passing houses on your left in Manhood Lane, turn left along signed Mill Lane to reach the pub. **Sat Nav:** PO20 7NB.

Parking: At The Crab & Lobster, with permission, or considerately nearby beside the village street.

This good, level walk explores the inlet that now forms Pagham Harbour Nature Reserve, a haven for wildlife. Beginning beside what was once the busy quayside; the route heads east on paths alongside the inter-tidal saltmarsh and its lagoons where distant views of the sea will be seen. It may be worthwhile bringing binoculars to help spot the wildlife here. After rounding a headland, the halfway point of the route is met at Pagham Wall when the way leaves the saltmarsh behind and heads inland through a large wild flower meadow to meet Honer Farm. The route then turns

Sidlesham Quay

west and continues through more peaceful meadows as it makes its return to Sidlesham Quay. Due to the marshland terrain, the route is not suitable during the winter months.

THE PUB — **THE CRAB & LOBSTER** describes itself as a stunning hideaway on the South Coast. The pub offers a good selection of drinks from the bar and a fine dining experience in the restaurant. That of course is miles away from how the 350-year-old building began life in the village. Today's chef produces dishes sourced from  local farmers and Selsey fishermen. The emphasis is on fresh fish that of course includes crab and lobster as you would expect. There is a good choice of starters while the more adventurous with larger appetites can plump for the delicious main courses. On a fine day, why not dine alfresco on the terrace amidst lovely views of the countryside?
⊕ crab-lobster.co.uk   ☎ 01243 641233

The Walk

1 From the pub, walk the few metres to the old quayside and turn left on a signed path besides a converted single-storey building. Now follow the path alongside the saltmarsh until a fork is met in 250 metres. Follow the left fork and continue with a hedgerow to your left. Soon ignore a signed path on the left and press on, always keeping the hedgerow to your left.

A century and a half ago the quay would have been a hive of activity with ships unloading grain for the large tide mill here. Although the mill has long gone, a couple of single-storey warehouses still exist. Life here changed in 1876 when the harbour entrance was sealed so that 700 acres of land could be reclaimed for farming only for the sea wall to be breached a few years later.

2 Ignore a second signed path on your left and continue ahead alongside the hedgerow. When the hedge bends left around a

West Sussex Pub Walks

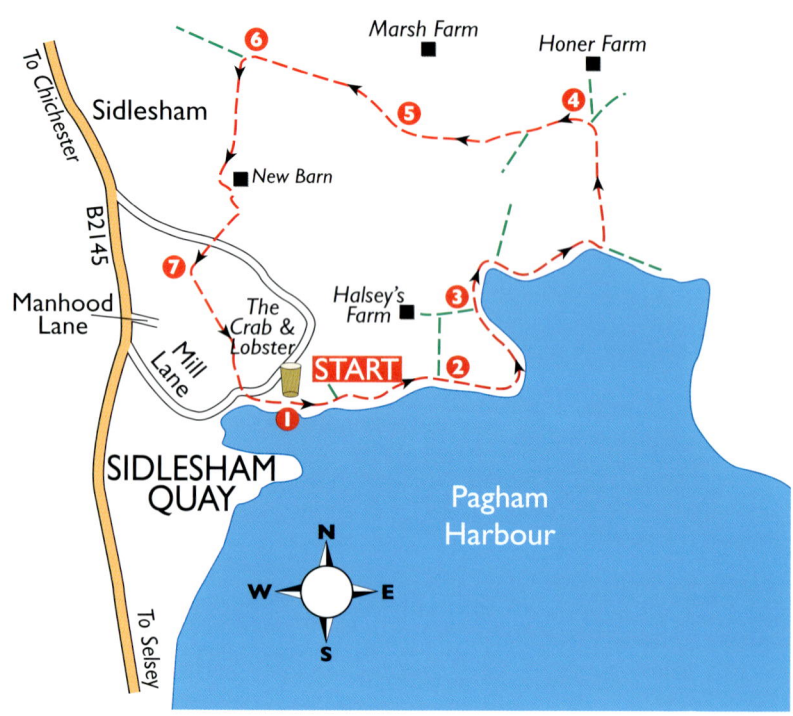

headland, remain on the path to the right of it and later cross a small ford. Soon press on along a narrow causeway between lagoons.

❸ At a junction of paths, go right along the causeway and pass an information board for **Halsey's Farm**. At a second directional post, turn right, again along a causeway. Soon after rounding a left bend a directional post is met. Turn left here down steps leaving the water's edge. Go ahead over a stile and plank bridge to enter a wild flower meadow. Now go ahead to the far top left corner and a gate.

❹ Go through the gate, ignore a stile ahead and turn left along the top edge of a meadow. Pass through a field gate and go ahead on a grassy path that begins to bend leftwards and meets a pedestrian gate. Pass through a ribbon of woodland to meet a second gate and cross a bridge.

Sidlesham Quay 5

5 Press on now crossing a large meadow and at its end pass through a gap in the hedgerow ahead of you. Maintain direction ahead; go under power cables and pass by a gate. Press on and cross a stile beside a gate in the tree line ahead of you to meet a concrete farm drive.

6 Continue along the drive and after 250 metres turn left on a path shared by cyclists. The path leads between arable fields, passes a barn and eventually ends at a road. Go diagonally right to a signed path and cross a sheepfold to a directional post ahead of you.

7 Turn left here with a hedgerow on your right and soon continue on a fenced path that later narrows and passes between gardens before ending back at the quayside where the pub will be found a few metres to your left.

Place of Interest Nearby

Chichester Cathedral was founded in 1075 and contains a couple of features that are unique; a free-standing medieval bell tower and double aisles, while the interior has rare medieval sculptures as well as modern artworks. The cathedral is in the centre of Chichester. **Sat Nav:** PO19 1PX.
⊕ chichestercathedral.org.uk ☎ 01243 782595

Walk 6

HALFWAY BRIDGE

Distance: 6 miles (9.6 km)

Map: OS Explorer OL33 Haslemere & Petersfield
Grid Ref: SU932219

How to get there: Halfway Bridge is signed north from the A272 midway between Petworth and Midhurst. **Sat Nav:** GU28 9BP.

Parking: Roadside parking near the front of the pub. Please park considerately.

This excellent walk begins in the small community that derives its name rather unimaginatively from the bridge nearby and unsurprisingly, is halfway between Petworth and Midhurst. The hamlet is sited within the glorious Sussex Downs Area of Outstanding Natural Beauty which offers miles of good country walks. After leaving the hamlet behind the route soon passes through pretty Lodsworth village before crossing Cowdray Park. The way then heads north on a not-too-strenuous climb that offers wonderful pastoral views before reaching Vining Farm from where the route begins its return. After passing back through Lodsworth the way rejoins the outward path before ending back at Halfway Bridge.

Halfway Bridge   6

THE PUB — **THE HALFWAY BRIDGE INN** began life as an 18th-century coaching inn and nowadays provides comfortable accommodation for guests to which the owners have added a fully equipped shepherds' hut in the grounds. The inn, with its honey-coloured walls and wisteria, exudes a relaxing atmosphere; just right after a country walk. The restaurant offers a good selection of freshly cooked local produce from burgers, filled ciabatta and sandwiches to Thai-style crispy sea bass. The owners also own the Crab & Lobster in Pagham Harbour that features in walk 5 of this book.
🌐 halfwaybridge.co.uk   ☎ 01798 861281

The Walk

1 With the pub at your back, go ahead on a bridleway between two houses. When the tarmac ends press on along the bridleway that later enters a field, fork left after 50 metres on a narrow path. At the field end keep ahead to meet the lychgate of **St Peter's church**. Turn left on the lane to meet **The Street**. Turn right along the road to a small green on your left. Turn left along the lane passing the end of **School Lane**. At a sharp left bend by **Heath End Farm**, go ahead on a bridleway that meets a T-junction. Turn

West Sussex Pub Walks

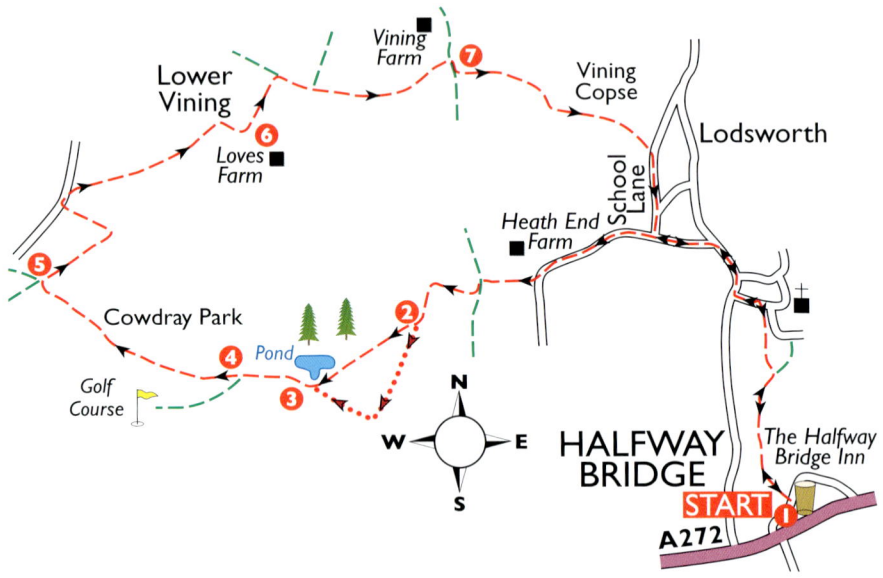

left and in 65 metres turn right to enter a field. Go ahead along the field edge and, at its corner, turn left along its edge until an easily missed kissing gate is met on your right.

2 The responsible landowner puts a sign on this gate if a bull is in the field. *If the sign is showing follow plan B.* If the sign is not showing, pass through the gate and cross this large field along an avenue of newly planted lime trees, later passing Steward's Pond and the Queen Elizabeth I oak, believed to be 800-1,000 years old, to meet a second kissing gate.

Plan B. Ignore the kissing gate and continue alongside the field edge, turning right at its end. Now follow a path that shadows the field on your right to meet with a kissing gate on your right.

3 If you have crossed the field, turn right after passing through the gate or, if using plan B, continue ahead from this gate. The path soon bends left and, on a rise, ignore a path signed left and press on to meet a golf course.

4 With caution, go ahead over the fairway to a footpath sign under a small oak tree. Now keep ahead following another couple of

Halfway Bridge 6

signposts to eventually leave the golf course and pass through a ribbon of trees to meet a field.

5 Turn right along the field edge and, at its end, turn left along its edge. At the corner, bear right and follow a path between hedgerows and along a driveway to meet a road beyond. Turn right along the road and in 12 metres turn right again and follow a rising driveway leading to **Lower Vining Farm**. Later, pass by the entrance to **Loves Farm** and soon after that of **Lower Vining Barn**. Keep ahead on a gravel track that soon bends right and ends at a field.

6 Turn left along the field edge to meet a T-junction with a wide path. Turn right and when a cart track is reached, ignore a path signed left and press on ahead. When the cart track bends right by a paddock, go ahead on a signed path that forks left before a gate is met and ends at a sunken bridleway.

7 Turn right here and in 80 metres turn left on a cart track that is soon joined by another from the left. Continue along the track that ends at **School Lane**. Go ahead along the road until a T-junction with the lane walked earlier is met where a left turn brings you to the small village green.

8 Retrace your earlier steps now by turning right along **The Street** and then left into **Church Lane**. Turn right at the church lychgate and go ahead, first on the footpath and then ahead on the bridleway to bring this scenic circuit to an end.

Place of Interest Nearby

Petworth House is a 17th-century mansion displaying an amazing collection of art and sculpture while the servants' quarters offer a glimpse of life below stairs. The 700-acre deer park was designed by Capability Brown and offers lovely views. Owned by the National Trust, the house is open from 11am to 5pm while the gardens, café and shop are open from 10am until 5pm. Church St, Petworth. **Sat Nav:** GU28 0AE
🌐 nationaltrust.org.uk/petworth-house-and-park
☎ 01798 342207

Walk 7
Heyshott

Distance: 4¼ miles (6.8 km)

Map: OS Explorer OL8 Chichester, South Harting & Selsey
Grid Ref: SU899179

How to get there: Heyshott is 3 miles south-east of Midhurst. From Midhurst follow the A286 southward for 2 miles before turning left into Bex Lane signed to Heyshott and The Unicorn Inn. Follow the brown tourist signs to the pub.
Sat Nav: GU29 0DL.

Parking: At The Unicorn Inn, with permission, or considerately at the roadside nearby.

Heyshott is a lovely spread out village below the escarpment of the South Downs and is perhaps better known for its Bonfire Night celebrations; said to be the best in Sussex. Two long-distance footpaths pass close to the village and both will be dipped into during this walk. The route begins by following a

Heyshott

quiet country lane that offers great views and brings you to the outskirts of Cocking. Here the way turns south on a steady uphill climb to join the South Downs Way that continues up Manorfarm Down. Surrounded by magnificent views, the route meets the New Lipchis Way long-distance path at Heyshott Down, an area managed to encourage wild orchids and butterflies. From here, the path descends very steeply down the escarpment before crossing fields to rejoin the village below.

THE PUB

THE UNICORN INN is just brimming with quintessential rural charm that makes pubs in the heart of the South Downs National Park so appealing. The interior has beamed ceilings that create a good cosy atmosphere while the beer garden is charming and has superb views over the adjoining countryside, all of which will entice you to relax and put your feet up on a sunny afternoon with a glass or two after this good country walk. From the pumps come ever-changing real ales that include Arundel Brewery's  Sussex Gold, Andwell Brewing Co's Gold Muddler and Adnams Lighthouse. A wide range of snacks, starters and hearty main courses are always available. Open all day except Sundays and Mondays when the hours are 12noon to 6pm.
🌐 unicorn-inn-heyshott.co.uk ☎ 01730 813486

The Walk

1 With your back to the pub, go left along the village street to meet a small road junction on a bend opposite the church. Turn left here along the road that, after passing **Leggs Farm**, becomes just a single track road. After ½ a mile this little-used road meets a T-junction.

2 Turn right and continue along this quiet road for 1 mile and soak up the lovely views it offers. After passing **Sunwool Farm**, ignore a signed footpath to the left and press on to meet a byway on your left by railings.

West Sussex Pub Walks

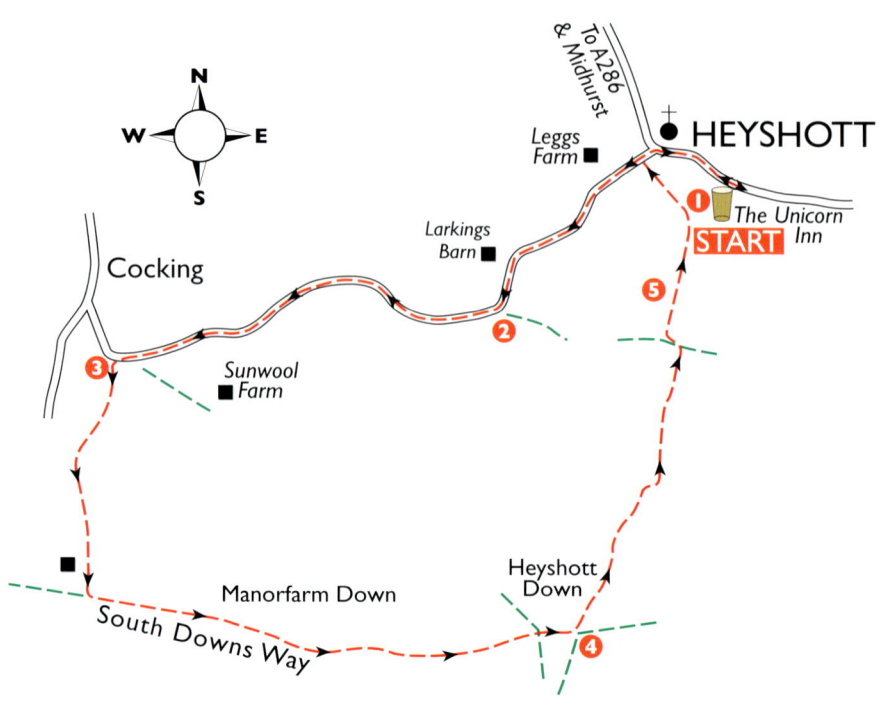

③ Turn left on this byway that begins to climb the Downs. After ½ mile the byway passes barns and ends at the **South Downs Way**. Turn left here along the long-distance path and continue up the Downs for 1 mile. When at the top of the hill, ignore a signed crossing footpath and press on ahead for 150 metres to meet a second direction post on a bend.

④ Turn left through a gate on a signed bridleway and cross a meadow to a gate opposite. Now continue on the path that descends steeply through woodland.

The unusual topography on the slopes to your right is due to chalk quarrying. The disused chalk pits have been re-colonised by downland grasses, orchids and horseshoe vetch which attract many butterflies.

The path finally ends by a gate with a track to your left. Turn left

Heyshott 7

along the track to meet a T-junction with another. Turn left for 50 metres before turning right on a signed footpath and cross the centre of a larger field aiming for an oak tree at the other side.

5 Pass by the oak tree and press on along the right side of the field to its corner and pass through a hedgerow to enter the next field. Although a fingerpost directs you diagonally left across this field, it is best to follow the field edge to meet a gate. Both ways end here. Go ahead to the left of a building to meet the lane walked earlier. Turn right along the lane and right again at the road junction to meet **The Unicorn Inn** and the end of this good walk.

Place of Interest Nearby

The ruins of **Cowdray House** are 3 miles north of Heyshott along the A286 at Midhurst. The house was built replacing an earlier one in the 1520s but was sadly destroyed by a ruinous fire during restoration work in 1793. The ruins are so important architecturally that they have been granted Grade I listing. In its day the building was one of England's greatest country houses and was said to be comparable with many palaces of its time.
Sat Nav: GU29 0AY. ⊕ cowdray.co.uk/historic-cowdray
☎ 01730 812423

Walk 8

LURGASHALL

Distance: 3½ miles (5.6 km)

Map: OS Explorer OL33 Haslemere & Petersfield
Grid Ref: SU937271

How to get there: Lurgashall is signed west off the A283, 5 miles north of Petworth. **Sat Nav:** GU28 9ET.

Parking: Limited at The Noah's Ark, so alternatively park around the village green.

Lurgashall is an attractive village lying in the shadow of Blackdown Hill that straddles the Surrey/Sussex border south of Haslemere. The village is ancient and still retains its popular cricket green that fronts The Noah's Ark public house while set back a little is the 13th-century church of St Laurence. The most famous resident of the village was Alfred, Lord Tennyson who enjoyed walking in the area. This undulating route, through a fine variety of fields and woodland, climbs the lower slopes of Blackdown Hill that Tennyson once enjoyed before heading east through fields with fantastic views. Turning once again, the way

Lurgashall 8

follows paths down gentle slopes beside woodland to meet a lovely track that returns you to The Noah's Ark and welcome refreshment.

THE PUB | **THE NOAH'S ARK** sits beside the picture postcard village green at Lurgashall and dates back to the 16th century. It is thought to get its name from the time when a water-filled ditch surrounded the building that was then a brewery and entry was via a gangplank, rather like boarding a ship. For several centuries the pub also baked bread leading to the local rhyme *'For well-baked bread and home-brewed ale, you must come to Lurgashale'*. The traditional interior is welcoming and cosy while tables are set out on the lawn to the front. The beers from the pumps feature IPA, Abbot Ale and constantly changing guest ales. The food has been featured in Michelin and AA guides which makes it important to book first if you wish to eat in the restaurant.

🌐 noahsarkinn.co.uk   ☎ 01428 707346

The Walk

1 When facing the pub, go left alongside the village green. Thirty metres after the green ends, turn right through a kissing gate. Now follow a well-trodden path through orchards and more kissing gates to reach woodland. Remain on the path as it leads you between the trees.

2 At the end of woodland, cross a stile and continue ahead on the wide path. Fork right by posts to meet a drive and continue along it until you reach a country lane. Turn left along the lane to meet a private drive on your right with the **Blackdown Distillery**, a few metres ahead of you.

3 Turn right along the drive and, at gates beside a gatehouse, press on ahead along the rising drive with **Blackdown Hill** ahead of you. Then, 80 metres before the gates of **Blackdown House** are

West Sussex Pub Walks

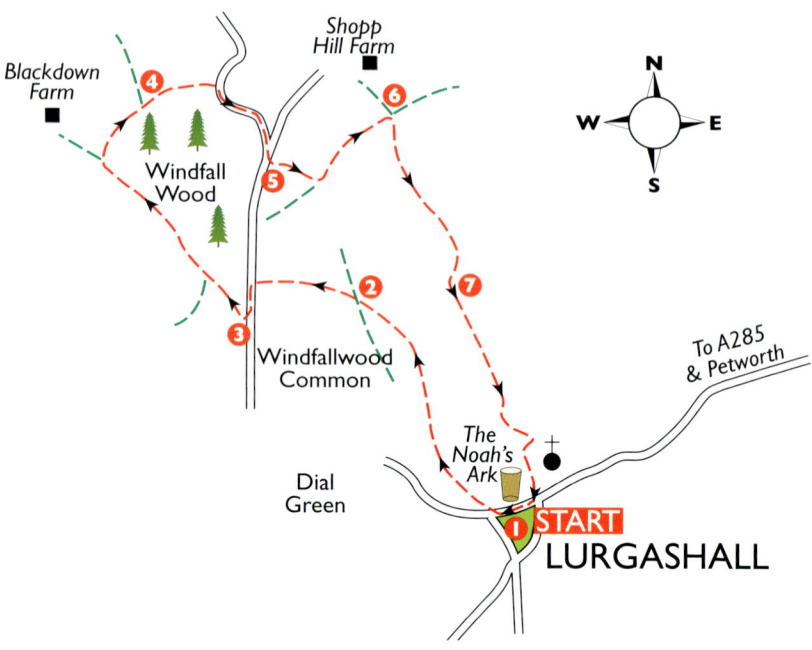

met, fork right on a rough drive and soon fork right again by a barn and pass the frontage of a large house.

4 Pass by a couple of more modest houses and ignore a path signed left. Go ahead into woodland and in 50 metres fork right and remain on this path when it enters a gully, crosses a bridge and climbs steps to meet with a narrow country lane. Follow the lane rightwards to meet a road junction.

5 Go ahead along the road and, in 60 metres, turn left along the drive of **Hobstevens Farm**. Follow the drive right to a log store and then go ahead and left to a footpath sign beside a field and pedestrian gate. Pass through the gate and go towards the bottom right corner of the field and another footpath sign. Cross a stile; ignore the path ahead of you and follow one signed to your left that leads to the far right corner of the field.

6 Go through a pedestrian gate; pass through a ribbon of woodland over a brook and climb steps to enter a field. Go ahead with a

Lurgashall 8

hedgerow to your right to meet a directional post. Turn right over a stile and go ahead through the centre of a large field. As you cross the brow of the hill, aim for a gate at the far side. Pass through this and press on ahead through the next field to a stile beside a field gate to meet a farm track.

7 Turn right along the track. On a right bend in the track, fork left over a stile and follow a narrow path ahead. Pass through a gate to meet a drive. Turn right between lily ponds and, at a junction of drives, go left through a field gate. Pass along the left side of a meadow to enter the graveyard of **St Laurence's church**. Bear right to exit the gate to rejoin **The Noah's Ark** and the end of this good circuit.

Place of Interest Nearby

The **Blackdown Distillery** (formerly the Lurgashall Winery) is only a few metres off the route or 1 mile west of the pub if travelling by car. The nearby woodland is dotted with silver birch trees that are tapped for their sap, an important ingredient in the various liqueurs, meads and spirits that are brewed and sold here. You are able to 'taste before you buy'. Open Tuesday to Friday 11am to 5pm and Saturdays 9am to 5pm. Jobsons Lane, Lurgashall. **Sat Nav:** GU28 9HA.
⊕ blackdowncellar.co.uk   ☎ 01428 707654.

Arundel Castle viewed from the route

Walk 9
Burpham

Distance: 4½ miles (7.2 km)

Map: OS Explorer OL10 Arundel & Pulborough
Grid Ref: TQ039089

How to get there: Burpham is signed off the A27 at Crossbush, 1 mile east of Arundel. Follow the road until it ends in Burpham beside the pub. **Sat Nav:** BN18 9RR.

Parking: None at The George at Burpham, so park in the clearly marked car park by the cricket ground left of the pub.

The lovely village of Burpham is at the end of a road that winds along the valley of the river Arun and because it is not a through route for motorists, the village remains as peaceful as it was a century ago. This varied route leaves the village via a quiet lane and soon passes its close neighbour, Wepham before climbing up New Down as it heads for the Monarch's Way long-distance path. The route then loses height as it continues along a peaceful valley floor below the slopes of Warningcamp Hill on its way to the bank of the river Arun and splendid views towards Arundel

Burpham

Castle. The riverbank is then followed back to Burpham where a climb up Jacob's Ladder, on a Saxon earthwork, soon returns you to the pub.

THE PUB — **THE GEORGE AT BURPHAM** is a friendly and welcoming pub thought to have been built back in the 1730s and is at the heart of the village opposite the Saxon church. Originally called The George and Dragon, the name change came recently when locals bought it to save it not only for themselves, but also for the many walkers visiting this stunning area. Since then it has thrived by selling good local real ales and modern seasonal cooking. The villagers' efforts have been rewarded by winning a 'Community Pub Award' and being a finalist in the 'Best Pub in Sussex 2016' competition. Open from 10.30am to 3pm and 6pm to 11pm weekdays and 10.30am until 11pm on weekends.
🌐 georgeatburpham.co.uk ☎ 01903 883131

The Walk

1 The route begins by walking back down the village street to a left bend and road junction. Turn right here along a narrow lane that descends into a shallow valley and up the other side to meet a road junction in the hamlet of **Wepham**.

2 Turn right along the road for 50 metres before turning left on a farm drive beside **Wepham Cottage**. Follow the drive uphill until it bends left by the farm gate. Turn right here on a downhill track signed as a bridleway.

3 At a T-junction by the foot of the slope the route now joins the **Monarch's Way** long-distance path. Turn right here, and at a fork in 90 metres, follow the right fork through a pedestrian gate and continue along the valley floor. Along the way, ignore a signed footpath to your left but look out for a second directional post soon after.

West Sussex Pub Walks

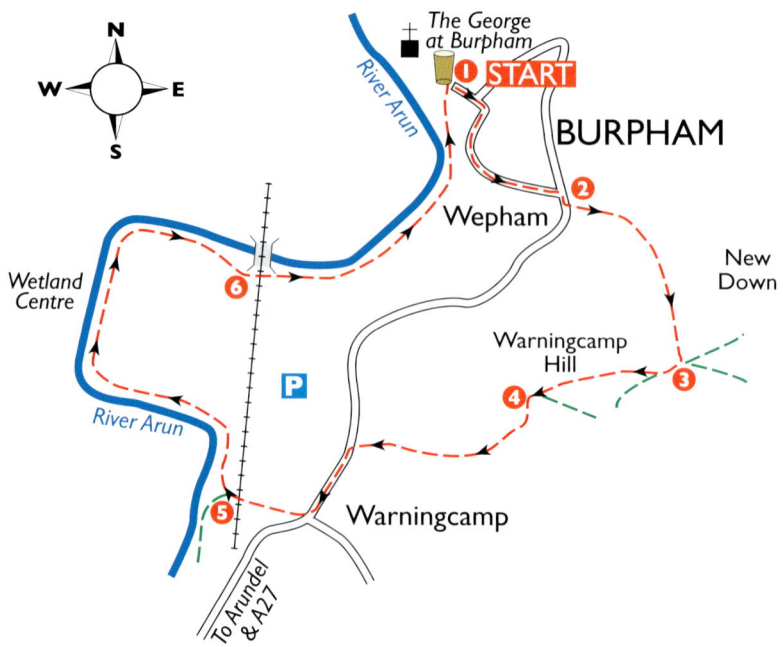

4 Fork left here to a third post where you should then fork right, still following the signed **Monarch's Way**. Keep to the well-trodden path that leads through peaceful woodland and ends at a road. Turn left along the road and continue on it until a road junction is met with a bus stop ahead of you. Turn right along a private road that ends at a gate with a railway line beyond. Take notice of the Stop, Look and Listen sign and cross the railway line.

5 At the far side, go ahead and seek out an easily missed path to the left of a cart track that leads rightwards along the river bank. If you miss it just follow the cart track and at its end go left up the bank and continue alongside the river. Keep to the riverside path until a railway bridge is met in 1½ miles.

6 Fork right to a railway crossing and again be aware of the Stop, Look and Listen signs before crossing to the far side. Go ahead through a field to its far left corner; cross a stile and go left up steps to rejoin the river bank and press on alongside the river.

Burpham

Finally, after ½ a mile the path narrows and meets a stile. Cross the stile and go ahead up the steps of **Jacob's Ladder**. At the top continue on a fenced path to rejoin the cricket ground with the pub just beyond.

As well as the Saxon church opposite the pub, part of the village itself sits on an ancient Saxon burgh. This earthwork fortification held a commanding position in its day, overlooking a bend in the River Arun, then an important waterway.

Place of Interest Nearby

WWT Arundel Wetland Centre is adjacent to the River Arun and offers safaris on electric boats through the naturalised wetlands where you may spot water voles or rare geese. Explore the secluded paths to spot wildlife or enjoy the great views from the café. Open each day from 9.30am until 5.30pm. Follow the brown duck signs from Arundel to the free onsite car park in Mill Road, Arundel. **Sat Nav:** BN18 9PB.
⊕ wwt.org.uk/wetland-centres/arundel   ☎ 01903 883355

Although Houghton Bridge looks medieval it was built in 1875

Walk 10
AMBERLEY

Distance: 6 miles (9.6 km)

Map: OS Explorer OL10 Arundel & Pulborough
Grid Ref: TQ025117

How to get there: Amberley is signed from the A29 Whiteways Lodge roundabout north of Arundel. Follow the B2139 for 2 miles to meet the pub on the right immediately after crossing Houghton Bridge. **Sat Nav:** BN18 9LR.

Parking: At The Bridge Inn, with permission, or limited parking at the roadside by Amberley Station.

Amberley 10

This undulating route begins on the outskirts of Amberley where it follows the bank of the River Arun to reach the hamlet of North Stoke. Here, the way meets a rising farm track that leads up the Downs on a not-too-difficult climb to reach an area known as The Burgh. With magnificent views over the countryside, the route then crosses a valley where, after climbing the far side, it heads northward to meet the attractive village of Amberley. Continuing along a pretty street dotted with thatched houses the route passes Amberley Castle; now a hotel. From here the route follows a grassy path over a couple of fields to re-join the bank of the river Arun which is then followed back to The Bridge Inn and the end of this good circuit.

THE PUB

THE BRIDGE INN is set on the outskirts of Amberley and backs onto the railway station and Amberley Chalkpit Working Museum for which it was once the quarry workers' 'beer shop'. Sited next to Houghton Bridge that crosses the River Arun here, The Bridge Inn offers an extensive menu of pub classics and daily specials including vegetarian options and a selection of real ales. The pub has been voted 'West Sussex Pub of the Year' recently and features regularly in CAMRA good beer guides and no wonder; with a pretty beer garden and patio for summer use and roaring log fires during the winter months it has much to offer. Closed Monday and Tuesday.

⊕ bridgeinnamberley.com ☎ 01798 831619

The Walk

1 From the pub, walk back to the B2139 and turn left alongside it with caution as there is no pavement. Very soon turn left on a signed footpath, cross a bridge over a stream to meet a stile which you should cross. Now go ahead along the riverside path for ¼ mile to reach a stile.

2 Cross the stile to meet a directional post in 50 metres. Turn left and follow a well-trodden path through a ribbon of woodland that ends at a quiet lane. Turn right along the lane to meet a T-junction by a telephone box.

West Sussex Pub Walks

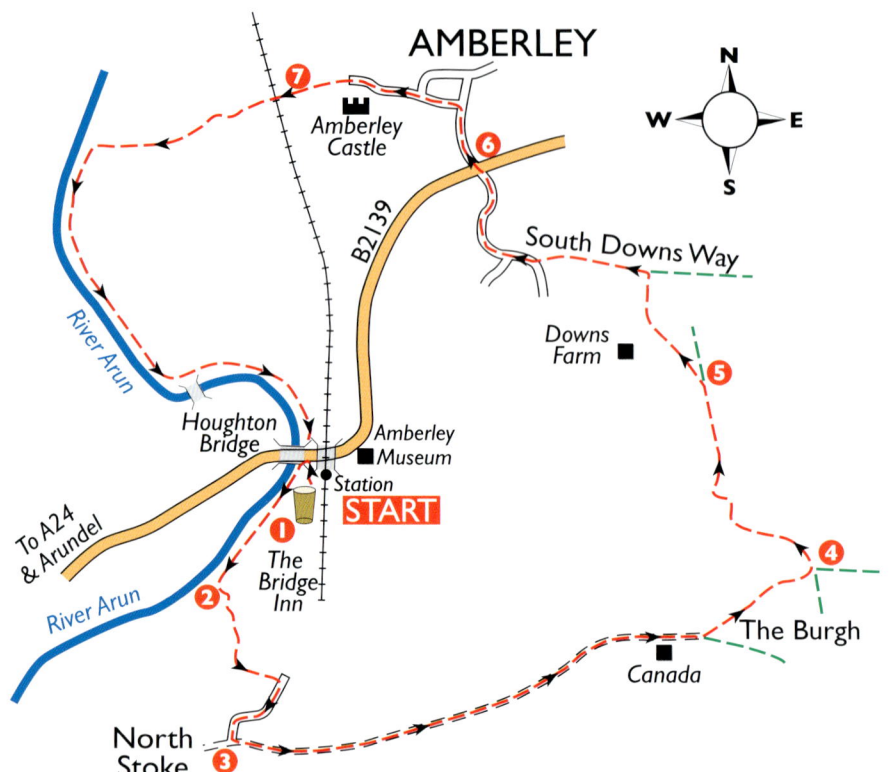

3 Turn left on a rising farm track later ignoring a crossing bridleway. After 1 mile pass by barns to your right that are oddly marked on OS maps as **Canada**. At a fork in 250 metres, you should fork left on a cart track. On a right bend, by a directional post, you should turn left on a signed bridleway.

4 Keep to the bridleway as it descends to the valley floor. Just before meeting a dew pond, follow the bridleway rightwards and pass through a gate at the field edge. Go left and continue on the signed bridleway as it climbs quite steeply out of the valley.

5 As the bridleway begins to level it meets a fork. Keep left here to soon join a chalk track and continue ahead to meet the signed **South Downs Way** path. Turn left along the SDW path which

Amberley 10

soon forks right and continues downhill to meet a country lane. Go ahead down the lane to meet the B2139.

6 With caution, cross the road and press on ahead passing the village school. At a road junction by the village tearooms, turn left and pass by pretty cottages and later **Amberley Castle** to reach the road end.

The castle was built during the 14th century by the Bishop of Chichester – it never saw conflict. The church next door is much older and dates from around 1100.

7 Go ahead on a path to reach a railway line. With care, and taking note of the Stop, Look & Listen sign, cross the line and press on along a grassy path through fields to rejoin the **River Arun**. Turn

West Sussex Pub Walks

left along its bank, later ignore a bridge and keep to the riverside path that skirts a caravan site to meet the B2139 with **The Bridge Inn** opposite.

Place of Interest Nearby

Amberley Museum & Heritage Centre is just the other side of the railway from The Bridge Inn and is a great place to visit. The 36-acre site has exhibits that include a narrow-gauge railway, nostalgic buses, a print workshop, blacksmith and potter. There are generally at least three crafts being demonstrated each day. Open from the second week in March until the end of October from Wednesday to Sunday and all week during West Sussex school holidays. ⊕ amberleymuseum.co.uk ☎ 01798 831370

Walk 11

Loxwood

Distance: 5½ miles (8.8 km)

Map: OS Explorer OL34 Crawley & Horsham
Grid Ref: TQ041311

How to get there: Loxwood is on the B2133, 6 miles north-west of Billingshurst. The pub is in the High Street beside the Wey & Arun Canal Visitor Centre. **Sat Nav:** RH14 0RD.

Parking: At The Onslow Arms, with permission, or in the public car park at the far end of the pub car park.

This wonderfully varied circuit begins and ends by walking the banks of the restored section of the Wey & Arun Canal. In between, the route heads north and passes through picturesque fields and shady woodland to meet and follow the Sussex Border Path. After walking a quiet lane utilised by the long-distance path, the way passes through the hamlet of Alfold Bars as it heads for the

West Sussex Pub Walks

newly restored Gennets Bridge over the canal that until recently was no more than a muddy ditch in the countryside. Thankfully, volunteers of the Way & Arun Trust have over the years produced sterling work on this previously un-restored section of the canal. The route now follows the canal bank for 1½ miles and brings you back to The Onslow Arms and welcome refreshment.

THE PUB — **THE ONSLOW ARMS** clientele two centuries ago were very different from those visiting today. Then it was boatmen that plied the waters of the canal passing its door while today's customers are more likely to be walkers and sightseers attracted to the restored scenic waterway. The popular 17th-century Grade II-listed building has oak beams, exposed brickwork and two gardens to enjoy during summer; one beside the canal and the other with a play area suitable for families, while in winter roaring log fires create a very cosy and comfortable atmosphere inside. A good selection of locally sourced food is on offer and the ales come from the Hall & Woodhouse brewery. Dogs welcome.
⊕ onslowarmsloxwood.com ☎ 01403 752022

The Walk

❶ From the pub, walk back to the road, turn right and right again on a signed bridleway between the canal bank and the pub garden. Press on along the canal bank passing a lock to reach a bridge.

❷ Turn left over the bridge and in 20 metres turn right on a signed footpath. Thirty metres after passing field gates on your left, turn left on a signed footpath across a plank bridge. Now follow a field edge until the path passes under power cables and enters woodland. Ignore a path forking right here and press on ahead through woodland to finally reach a road.

❸ Cross the road with caution and continue along the drive to **Barnsfold Cottage**. Follow the path around the rear of a barn and cross a stile. Go ahead along a field edge to a second stile and enter a ribbon of woodland. Soon the path bends right alongside a field. Now follow this path and ignore the occasional path signed to left and right.

Loxwood 11

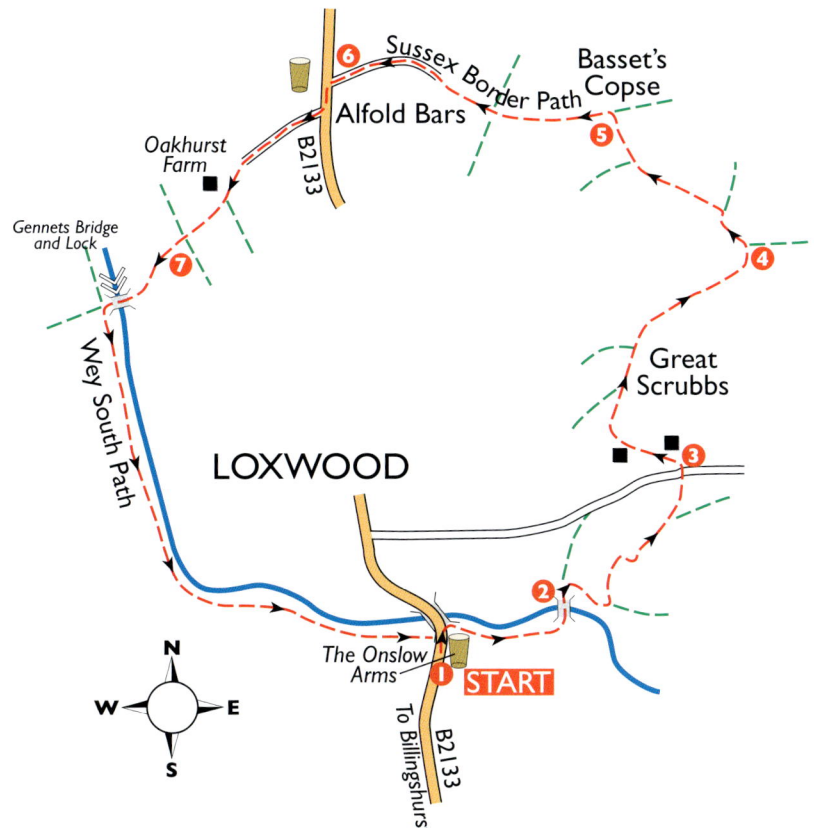

4 When a wide bridleway joins the path from the right, press on ahead. After crossing a bridge a T-junction is met. Turn right and, within a few metres, turn left on a signed footpath. Remain on the path now until it ends at a sunken T-junction with a bridleway.

5 This is the **Sussex Border Path** and the route now turns left along it. When a tarmac drive is met continue ahead along it passing farm buildings. Later the drive becomes a quiet country lane and ends at the B2133 road.

6 Cross the road with caution and go left along the grass verge to very soon meet **Oakhurst Lane**, signed as the Sussex Border

West Sussex Pub Walks

Path. Follow this quiet lane to meet the gates of **Oakhurst Farm**. Fork left through a pedestrian gate and continue on a farm track alongside a field. Keep on the track at a bend and at its end pass through a gate.

7 Ignore paths to left and right and press on ahead along a shady cart track to meet and cross newly built **Gennets Bridge** and lock to meet the **Wey South path**.

The Wey and Arun Canal was 23 miles in length and connected the River Wey at Shalford to the River Arun at Pallingham via 26 locks. The last barge to travel this section was in 1888. Interest in the canal was raised after P.A.L. Vine's book London's Lost Route to the Sea *was published in 1965. Enthusiasts banded together to begin the restoration work that continues today.*

Loxwood 11

Turn left along the canal bank here and follow it until it brings you back to **The Onslow Arms** to complete the walk. Along the way you will notice just how much restoration work the volunteers still have ahead of them.

Place of Interest Nearby

The **Wey & Arun Canal Trust** runs public narrowboat trips along the scenic Loxwood Link section of the restored canal close to the Surrey/Sussex border from the wharf behind the Onslow Arms.
⊕ weyarun.org.uk ☎ 01403 752403
(Mon – Fri 9.30am to 1.30pm).

Walk 12
BILLINGSHURST

Distance: 3¼ miles (5.2 km)

Map: OS Explorer OL34 Crawley & Horsham
Grid Ref: TQ072254

How to get there: Follow the A272 westward out of Billingshurst to meet the B2133 on a sharp right-hand bend. Turn left here to meet The Limeburners in 150 metres. **Sat Nav:** RH14 9JA.

Parking: At The Limeburners, with permission, or at the roadside.

This easy field walk is particularly lovely during spring and early summer when the meadows are brimming with wild flowers. The paths are well signed and easy to follow as the route makes its way along the floor of a shallow valley where the infant River Arun meanders on its way to the sea. The turning point of the walk comes when a pretty picnic site is met beside the now

Billingshurst 12

dry and deserted Lording's Lock on what was once the Wey & Arun Canal. From here, more field paths are followed that offer glorious panoramic views across the pastoral landscape with a distant backdrop of the South Downs. Near the end of the walk the way passes along the bank of a picturesque lake by Streele Farm before soon ending back at The Limeburners.

THE PUB

THE LIMEBURNERS is ideally situated in beautiful countryside on the outskirts of Billingshurst. The picture-book, family-run pub dates back to the 17th century when it began life as three workers' cottages, which is reflected in the low beams and country-style furnishings of the interior that create a cosy and welcoming atmosphere. To entice you further the pub offers a selection of Fuller's ales and fresh food from lunchtime snacks to something more substantial on the chef's 'specials' board. To the front is a pretty garden set out with tables while behind the pub is their own campsite if you wish to make a weekend of it. Closed Monday.
⊕ limeburnersbillingshurst.co.uk   ☎ 01403 782311

The Walk

❶ With your back to the pub, go left alongside the road; pass the campsite entrance and soon turn right on a private tree-lined drive signed as a public footpath. When the drive divides, go over a stile on your right and continue diagonally left across a meadow to a gate and stile ahead. Continue on a downhill grassy path to cross another stile and later a bridge to meet a junction of paths in 50 metres by a directional post.

❷ Turn left here, soon cross a footbridge and continue on a path alongside a large meadow with a hedgerow to your right. Follow the path as it enters woodland via a stile with the **River Arun** to your left and what was the **Wey & Arun Canal** on your right. The canal has attracted the name of London's Lost Route to the Sea

West Sussex Pub Walks

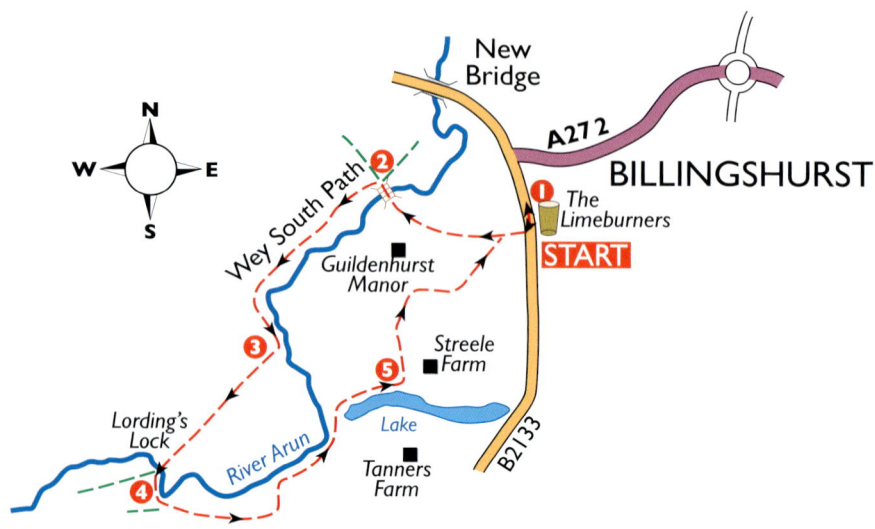

and unfortunately nowadays this section is now no more than a muddy ditch.

❸ The path ends at a stile and direction post. Turn right and continue alongside a large meadow with a hedgerow on your right. Towards the end of this path it becomes enclosed by willows and meets a stile. Here turn right to meet with the remains of **Lording's Lock**, its unique restored waterwheel and a couple of picnic tables.

Lording's Lock is unique in canal design as it forms an aqueduct over the River Arun that passes below. The restored waterwheel once raised water from the river to top up the canal.

❹ Pass the waterwheel, cross a weir and go through a kissing gate. Now follow a grassy path left to meet a direction post where the route swings leftwards alongside a meadow. Fifty metres after passing under power cables, turn left on a signed downhill path. Keep to this well-signed path that later follows the bank of a scenic lake.

❺ When a boathouse is reached, turn left on a path enclosed by hedgerows to meet a barn ahead of you. Follow a path to its left

Billingshurst 12

that skirts a field to meet, and pass through, two gates and enters a meadow. Follow the path diagonally right and, at its end, pass through a gate and kissing gate to rejoin the private drive walked earlier. Turn right to meet the road and then left to rejoin **The Limeburners** and the end of this good walk.

Place of Interest Nearby

Parham House and Gardens was built in 1577 and since those early times it is said the tranquillity and timeless beauty has changed little. As well as the house and gardens there is The Big Kitchen Restaurant serving home-made cakes and dishes using produce from the gardens. Parham is 5 miles south of Billingshurst and is open from 1 April to 14 October on Wednesdays, Thursdays, Fridays, Sundays and Bank Holidays from 12noon until 5pm (house from 2pm to 5pm). The main entrance is on the A283 Pulborough to Storrington road.
Sat Nav: RH20 4HR.
⊕ parhaminsussex.co.uk   ☎ 01903 742021

Walk 13
RUDGWICK

Distance: 3 miles (4.8 km)

Map: OS Explorer OL34 Crawley & Horsham
Grid Ref: TQ090342

How to get there: Rudgwick is on the B2128 6 miles west of Horsham and signed north from the A281 Horsham to Guildford road. The pub is at the northern end of the village. **Sat Nav:** RH12 3EB.

Parking: At The Kings Head pub, with permission, or at the roadside nearby.

This super walk, up close to the Surrey/Sussex border, leads you easily through quiet and peaceful countryside without ever being too far from habitation. After passing through a wooded valley where a brook is crossed, the way continues over scenic fields to soon join with the Downs Link long-distance path. Here, the route heads south for a mile under the shade of the trees that line this super track. When the track meets with the busy A281

Rudgwick

the route turns back towards the village by following a lovely bridleway known as Bowcroft Lane. The entire route is very easy to follow and the trees that line much of the way offer welcome cool shade on a hot summer's day. The route ends by passing the glorious village church to meet the pub beyond.

THE PUB **THE KINGS HEAD** is another of the county's ancient pubs. The pub is unusually long and narrow due to it being built on a strip of land between the road and the village's Norman church. The building is mainly 18th-century although some parts are older. There is a good variety of ales; some brewed in the village itself while the food ranges from sandwiches to beer-battered cod and chips with plenty of choices in between. The bar has comfortable sofas and, during winter, wood-burning stoves glow in the bar and restaurant area while outside is a pretty flower-bedecked patio area. Closed Monday and Tuesday.
🌐 kingsheadrudgwick.co.uk ☎ 01403 822200

The Walk

1 The route begins by following a narrow path to the left of the pub car park entrance. The path passes through a small valley via steps and crosses a woodland brook to meet a field at the far side. Go ahead along the right-hand field edge and at a second field continue along its right side to cross a stile at its end. Press on ahead to soon meet a road.

2 Cross the road diagonally right to a signed public footpath, pass through a gate and press on ahead over the field aiming for a second gate at the far side.

Beyond the tree line on your right here is a clay pit where a unique discovery was made in 1985 when the fossilised bones of a dinosaur that once roamed the area 100 million years ago were uncovered. One of only three ever discovered; it is named Polacanthus Rudgwickensis.

West Sussex Pub Walks

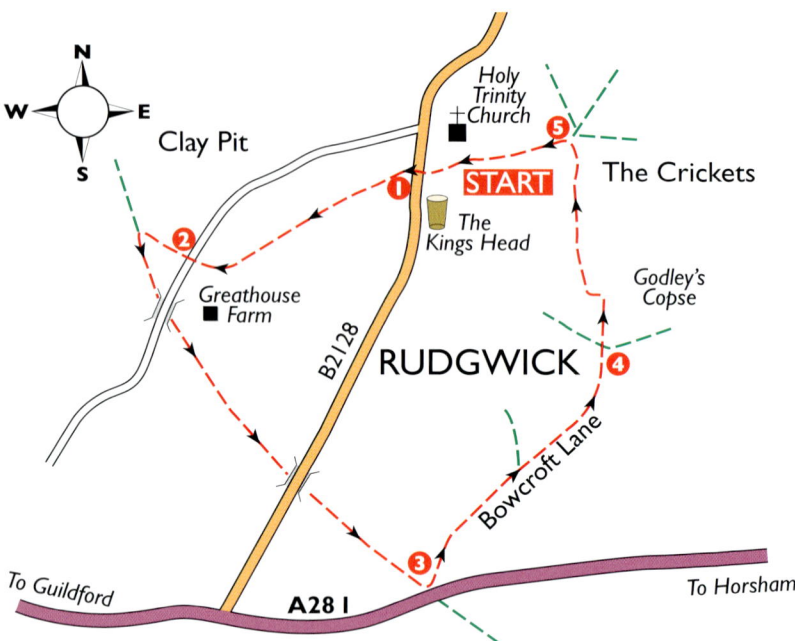

Pass through the gate to meet a crossing track. This is the **Downs Link** long-distance path and it is here that the route turns leftwards along it. This lovely path passes under two road bridges before finally meeting a gate after 1 mile with the A281 main road beyond.

❸ Pass the gate; go left for 10 metres before turning left again and with your back to the road follow a signed bridleway between trees. Now continue on this bridleway known as **Bowcroft Lane** and soon pass by a low, almost illegible memorial stone.

The memorial is to a local man; 2nd Lt Holford Secretan, who was killed in action in May 1940 during WWII.

When a wider track comes in from the right keep ahead. Soon, when this wider track bends left by a mounting block, press on ahead.

❹ Later ignore a crossing path. Soon after this, keep to the bridleway when it becomes fenced with a house to the left and a tennis court

Rudgwick

to the right. Follow the bridleway left at the end of the garden to meet the drive of the house. Here, turn right along the drive.

5 At a right bend in the drive with footpaths signed left and right; follow the left-hand path over a stile and continue ahead beside a line of trees before passing the side of a house. Go ahead along the drive, round a bend and turn right on a footpath across a small meadow to meet a churchyard. Pass to the left of the church to reach the pub and the end of this good walk.

Holy Trinity church dates back to 1270 and has an unusual marble font. Although the bell tower is 13th-century, the church itself was largely rebuilt during the 14th century.

Place of Interest Nearby

Hannah Peschar Sculpture Garden exhibits around 200 pieces of sculpture by over 50 artists each year in a garden designed by Anthony Paul that is a work of art itself. This unique environment changes throughout each season. Open Thursday to Saturday and Bank Holidays from 11am to 6pm from the end of March until the end of October and dogs are welcome. The garden is just over 5 miles north of Rudgwick at Black and White Cottage, Standon Lane, Ockley, Surrey. **Sat Nav:** RH5 5QR.
🌐 hannahpescharsculpture.com ☎ 01306 627269

13th-century Holy Trinity church is tucked away behind The Kings Head pub

Walk 14
Findon

Distance: 4 miles (6.4 km)

Map: OS Explorer OL10 Arundel & Pulborough
Grid Ref: TQ122088

How to get there: Findon is signed east off a roundabout on the A24, 3 miles north of Worthing. Go downhill to meet the The Square with the pub on your left. **Sat Nav:** BN14 0TE.

Parking: Very limited at The Village House, so use the small parking area in the road opposite the pub or park considerately alongside the village street.

Fortunately for Findon and its residents, the village was bypassed by the A24 main road back in 1938 and its centre seems to have remained untouched by time ever since. Findon nestles in a peaceful valley between the slopes of Cissbury Hill topped by its Iron Age fort to the east and Church Hill to the west. The route

Findon 14

soon leaves the village behind as it follows a track that gains height over open downland to meet No Man's Land – a strange name for this lovely countryside. The way then turns and follows the Monarch's Way long-distance path that leads easily back to Findon. Once away from the village, much of the route offers uninterrupted panoramic views across the countryside and as far as the sea in the south.

THE PUB

THE VILLAGE HOUSE is situated right in the heart of the village and the building has had a chequered life; from being a private house, a convalescent home, a guest house and tea room before finally becoming the fine pub and restaurant it is today. The bar boasts a variety of local real ales, premium spirits and wines. A selection of snacks is available as well as more substantial meals in the restaurant that include fish and chips for which they have earned a good reputation. Outside is an enclosed picturesque beer garden to relax in, where during summer weekends a barbeque is on offer.

🌐 villagehousefindon.co.uk ☎ 01903 873350

West Sussex Pub Walks

The Walk

❶ With your back to the pub cross the road, pass a small parking area to meet **Stable Lane** which heads off leftwards. Follow the rising lane until it finally ends by the gateway to **Gallops Farm**. Now follow a chalky byway rightwards that soon crosses the top of the Downs and offers fantastic views across the countryside and as far as the sea beyond. A feature of the landscape here to your right is **Cissbury Ring**.

Cissbury Ring is a huge Iron Age hillfort dating back to around 400BC. Later, the Romans occupied it and raised the ramparts. Surprisingly, during WWII it was once again used for military purposes when it was fortified with gun emplacements.

❷ After 1 mile, a vehicle barrier and a junction of tracks will be met. Ignore tracks to the left and right and press on ahead passing by a field gate. Finally the track descends into a valley and forks. Take the right fork that initially follows a fence line and, at the bottom of the slope, meet with a junction of tracks. This area is known as **No Man's Land**.

The name No Man's Land appears on some early tithe maps and generally marks a field or area where a number of undefined manorial

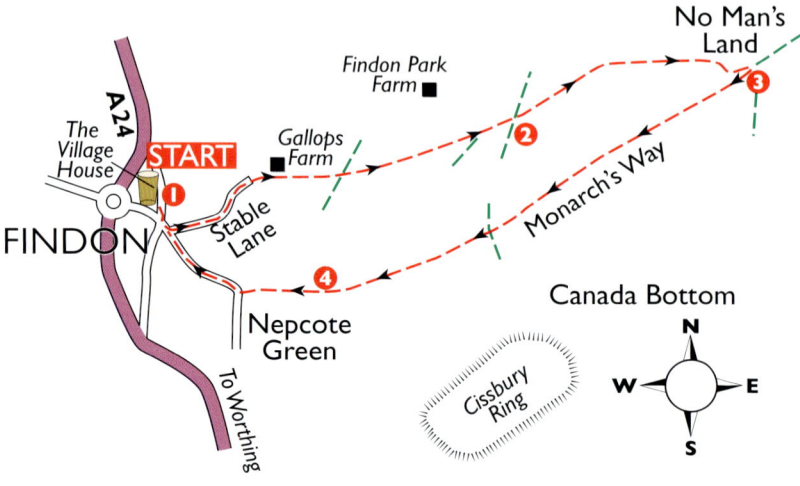

Findon 14

or parish boundaries meet. There is another No Man's Land marked on maps near High Salvington Windmill to the south of here.

③ Ignore all the tracks now and turn sharply right by a post, almost back on yourself on a narrow path signed as the **Monarch's Way** long-distance path. Remain on this narrow fenced path across the Downs, again with fantastic views, and later cross a wide chalky track before keeping ahead on the **Monarch's Way**.

④ After 1½ miles, the path ends at a lane beside **Ring House**. Press on ahead along the lane passing lovely **Nepcote Green** to meet a road junction. Go ahead here along **Nepcote Lane**, a quiet tree-lined residential road that leads back to the **Village House** and the end of this scenic walk.

Place of Interest Nearby

High Salvington Windmill, also known as Durrington Windmill, is a Grade II-listed post mill of 1750 sited 320 ft above sea level on the outskirts of Worthing. Restored to full working order in 1991 and run by volunteers, the mill is open on the first and third Sundays of each month from 2.30pm to 5pm from April until September. Light refreshments and a shop are on site. The windmill is 3½ miles south of Findon in Furze Road, High Salvington, Worthing. **Sat Nav:** BN13 3BP.
⊕ highsalvingtonwindmill.co.uk .

Beeding Bridge from the riverbank

Walk 15
BRAMBER

Distance: 2½ miles (4 km)

Map: OS Explorer OL11 Brighton & Hove **Grid Ref:** TQ188106

How to get there: Bramber is off the A283, 3 miles north of the A27 at Kingston by Sea. The Castle Inn Hotel is in Bramber's main street. **Sat Nav:** BN44 3WE.

Parking: At The Castle Inn Hotel, with permission, or in the small car park opposite.

This easy-to-follow short walk begins in the heart of Bramber and very soon passes the ruins of Bramber Castle that dates back to the 10th century and, although not much exists today

Bramber 15

it still makes a fascinating spot to explore. Leaving the castle grounds, the route meets the Downs Link long-distance path that leads away from the village as it passes by fields with glorious views to join with the bank of the River Adur. Here, the route begins its return on a lovely riverside path where there is a chance of seeing a little egret or two wading in the shallows. After meeting Beeding Bridge the route returns along the interesting village street to rejoin the pub. The walk is eminently suitable for all times of the year, even after heavy rain as it follows all-weather paths.

THE PUB

THE CASTLE INN HOTEL dates back to the 17th century although a coaching inn has stood on this site since the 13th century. The hotel is described as a typically English village inn brimming with 'olde worlde' charm. The comfortable bar supports a good variety of ales, wines and spirits while the daily menu constantly changes but always includes a range of sandwiches, platters, classic pub meals and the chef's specials. On fine summer days relax in a comfortable chair on the patio or at a table in the picturesque garden that comes complete with a shimmering brook. Although not seen in the picture, during the summer months the hotel's frontage is hidden behind a multitude of flower-bedecked window boxes and colourful hanging baskets.
⊕ castleinnhotel.co.uk ☎ 01903 812102

The Walk

❶ With your back to the pub, turn left along the pavement and soon, for a short excursion to the castle ruins, turn right across the road to steps opposite **The Old Tollgate Hotel**. Pass the lychgate of **St Nicholas' Church** and follow the path rightwards to meet the castle grounds.

The castle was built soon after the Norman Conquest and is perched on a natural knoll overlooking the River Adur and a gap in the South Downs. Subsidence during the 16th century, rather than war, caused its demise. The holes in the 14-metre high remaining wall are joist slots and indicate how many floors the keep had.

West Sussex Pub Walks

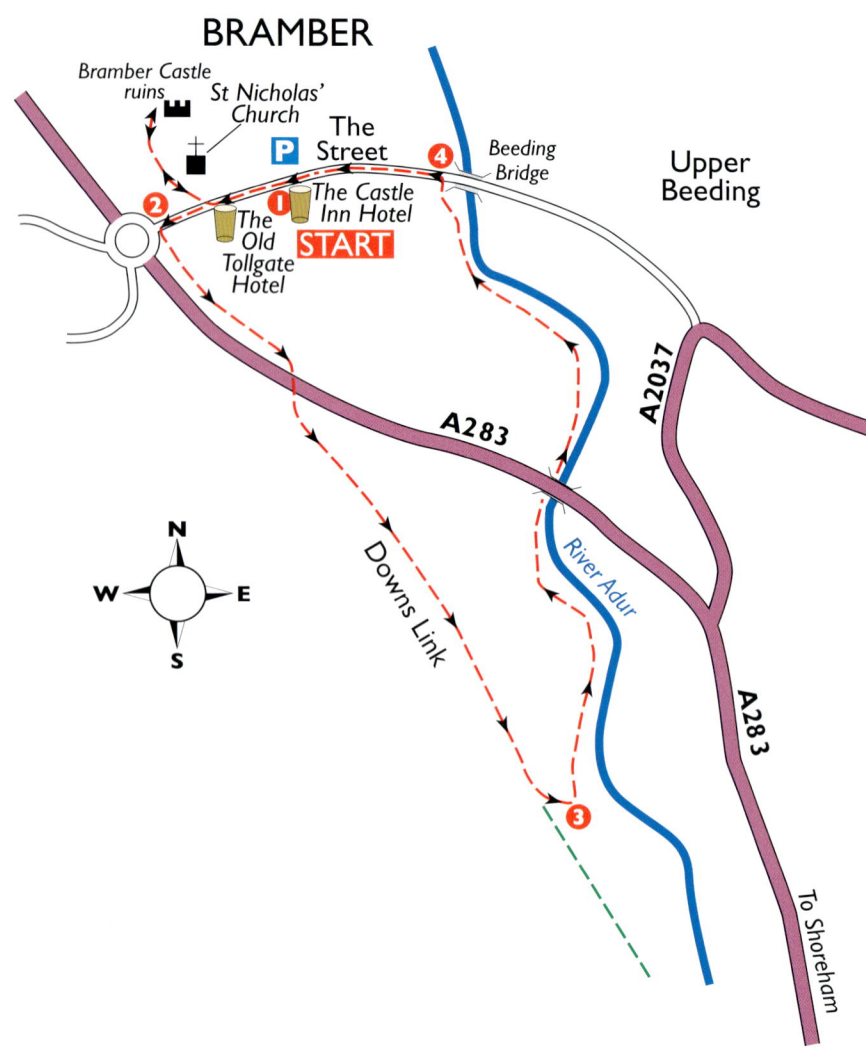

2 Return to the road and continue rightwards along the pavement until a roundabout is soon met. Here turn left on the signed **Downs Link** path that for a while shadows the road. Turn right at a sign directing the Downs Link path towards **Shoreham**, cross the road and press on along the path following signs to Shoreham until the bank of the **River Adur** is met.

Bramber 15

❸ Now turn left along the riverside path and ignore all other paths. Continue alongside the water's edge, pass under a road bridge and press on to meet **Beeding Bridge** where you should climb steps to meet the village street.

❹ Turn left along the street passing by **St Mary's House** along the way to soon rejoin the pub to complete this good short walk.

St Mary's House was built in 1470 by William Waynflete, Bishop of Winchester and used as an inn for pilgrims on their way to the tomb of St Thomas of Canterbury. It is believed that King Charles II stayed here during his escape after the Battle of Worcester in 1651, the last battle of the English Civil War.

West Sussex Pub Walks

Place of Interest Nearby

Steyning Museum tells the story of the local area from ancient times to the present day. There are permanent exhibits and temporary displays that make the museum well worth a visit. Open 10.30am to 4pm Tuesday, Wednesday, Friday and Saturday (Sunday 10am to 4pm). The museum is just over 1 mile north-west of Bramber at 32 Church Street, Steyning. **Sat Nav:** BN44 3YB.
⊕ steyningmuseum.org.uk ☎ 01903 813333

The remains of Bramber Castle

Walk 16
RUSPER

Distance: 4½ miles (7.2 km)

Map: OS Explorer OL34 Crawley & Horsham
Grid Ref: TQ205373

How to get there: Rusper is 5 miles north-west of Crawley and is signed north from the A264 Crawley to Horsham road. The pub is in the High Street opposite the church. **Sat Nav:** RH12 4PX.

Parking: None at the pub so use the village car park beside the church.

This lovely walk begins by following the Sussex Border Path westward out of Rusper to soon meet and pass through magnificent Horsegills Wood where streams and rivulets have

West Sussex Pub Walks

cut deep channels between the trees. After reaching a quiet lane, the route turns east and continues alongside woodland that offers fine pastoral views over the countryside. The way then heads for, and passes through outstanding Baldhorns Park where a bridleway leads to Rusper Court Farm before the route finally turns northwards and heads back to the village. It is a sheer wonder just how much wildlife can be seen from the route; deer are often grazing at the woodland edges while buzzards circle above giving out their high-pitched cry.

THE PUB **THE PLOUGH & ATTIC ROOMS** dates back to the 16th century and this welcoming pub comes with stone flag floors and very low beams. It is said the favourite pastime of locals is to watch visitors banging their heads! The pub was originally called The Plough but the modern appendage came in 2007 when the attic rooms on the first floor were opened as dining rooms. So, spoilt for choice, you can eat downstairs in the bar and lounge, or venture upstairs to the vaulted Attic Rooms. There is a wide range of food on offer that will suit all tastes. Outside is a large sunny garden just right for relaxing in after a country walk.
⊕ theploughandatticroomsrusper.com   ☎ 01293 871215

The Walk

❶ With your back to the car park entrance, go left along a path to reach a recreation ground. Turn left and pass along the left edge of the ground and go through a gate at its end. Follow the signed **Sussex Border Path** through meadows with a hedgerow to your left to meet woodland.

❷ Enter woodland and follow a well-trodden path. Look out for a marker post signed right where you should go down steps into a ravine, cross a bridge and climb out the other side. Continue on the path to meet a directional post where you should turn right and enter a field.

❸ Turn left along the field edge and, in its far corner, go through a kissing gate and press on along a path between trees. At a stile on your right enter a meadow and go ahead to a hedgerow before

Rusper 16

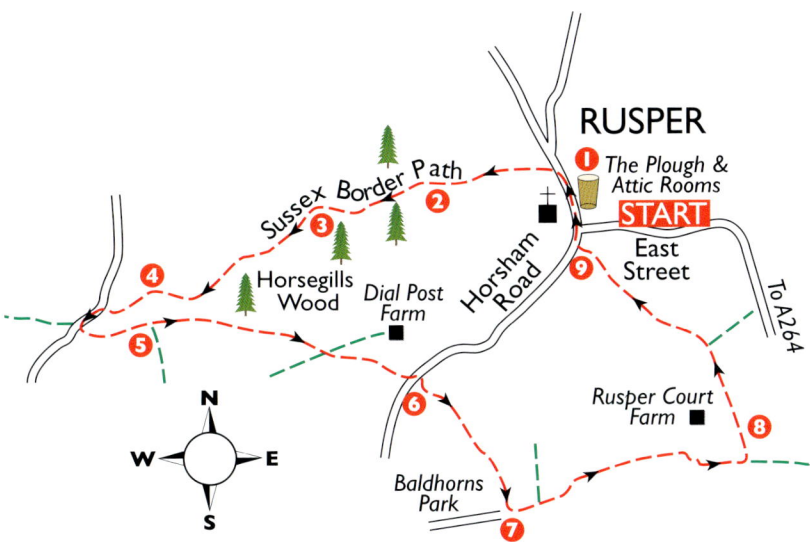

turning left alongside it to meet a stile on your right within it. Cross the stile and go left along a field edge and, at its end, pass a house to meet a drive.

4 Continue along the drive to soon meet and cross a stile on your left. Go diagonally right over a paddock, pass a field byre and cross a stile in the corner. Press on to soon meet a road. Turn left along the road and, at a left bend, ignore the **Sussex Border Path** to your right and turn left on a signed footpath through woodland.

5 Exit woodland via a gate and go ahead to a directional post in 35 metres. Ignore a path signed right and press on ahead. Later the grassy path meets with a cart track where you should continue ahead along it. At a directional post, ignore paths signed left and right and keep ahead. As you approach farm buildings fork right on a narrow path to meet a road.

6 Go left for 35 metres before turning right on a signed path alongside a field. At a directional post pointing diagonally right across the field to its far corner you have a choice. If a crop is

West Sussex Pub Walks

growing you may choose to continue along the field edge were the farmer has left a path. Both ways meet a directional post in the corner where you continue on a path over a brook in woodland before passing between the manicured grounds of **Baldhorns Park** and a tennis court to meet a drive.

7 Turn left along the drive signed as a bridleway. At the gates to **Winterfold Farm** follow the bridleway to their left. Keep to the bridleway that eventually meets and continues along a drive. In 80 metres, by a directional post, turn left along the drive to **Briar Cottage**.

8 Pass the cottage gate and fork left, cross a bridge and keep ahead along a field edge. At the top corner cross a plank bridge and stile

Rusper

on your right. Ignore a path signed right and go left on a grassy path through the centre of a meadow. At the top of the field press on between fences.

9 Pass between barns and continue ahead on a narrow path to the rear of gardens. Pass a pub car park to meet with a road and cross to the pavement opposite. Turn right along the pavement to soon rejoin the pub and car park.

Place of Interest Nearby

Horsham Museum and Art Gallery can be found in The Causeway, Horsham 4 miles south-west of Rusper. The museum is free and contains 26 galleries covering such things as fashion, local trade and prehistory and has been described as the Victoria & Albert Museum in miniature. Open from 10am until 4pm Tuesday to Saturday.
⊕ horshammuseum.org   ☎ 01403 254959

Walk 17
Nuthurst

Distance: 3½ miles (5.6 km)

Map: OS Explorer OL34 Crawley & Horsham
Grid Ref: TQ192262

How to get there: Nuthurst is 2 miles south of Mannings Heath. When travelling from Mannings Heath on the A281, fork right at Monk's Gate on the road signed to Nuthurst. The pub will be reached in 1¼ miles. **Sat Nav:** RH13 6LH.

Parking: At The Black Horse Inn, with permission or at the roadside nearby.

This wonderful woodland walk begins by following the pristine driveway of Cook's Farm before entering Lodgesale Wood where a bridleway leads between birch and pine trees that offer cool shade on a hot summer's day while the faint scent of pine hangs in the air. After crossing a country lane the route continues on another easily followed bridleway through more woodland before meeting its turning point where it crosses a field and follows a farm cart track to join Prings Lane. Here the way continues over more fields before passing through the shade of Boyds Wood to

Nuthurst

soon rejoin the outward path that leads back to The Black Horse Inn and the end of this walk. Some sections of the route may become muddy during winter.

THE BLACK HORSE INN began life as three 17th-century farm workers' homes as evidenced by the attached cottages that still display their ancient oak framing. The interior is welcoming with its stone floors, beamed ceilings and open fires that add to its charm and atmosphere. During summer, tables are set out in the lovely garden that comes with its own small stream. Food ranges from starters such as soup of the day through to the more substantial pub classics. The pub boasts many awards for its food which makes it essential that if wishing to eat here you should book first. Closed Monday.
⊕ theblackhorseinn.com ☎ 01403 891272

The Walk

1 With your back to the pub, go left along the road for 90 metres and then turn left on a signed footpath along the drive to **Cook's Farm**. As the drive bends left, and with a well manicured garden ahead of you, fork right on a signed bridleway that passes to the right of a barn.

West Sussex Pub Walks

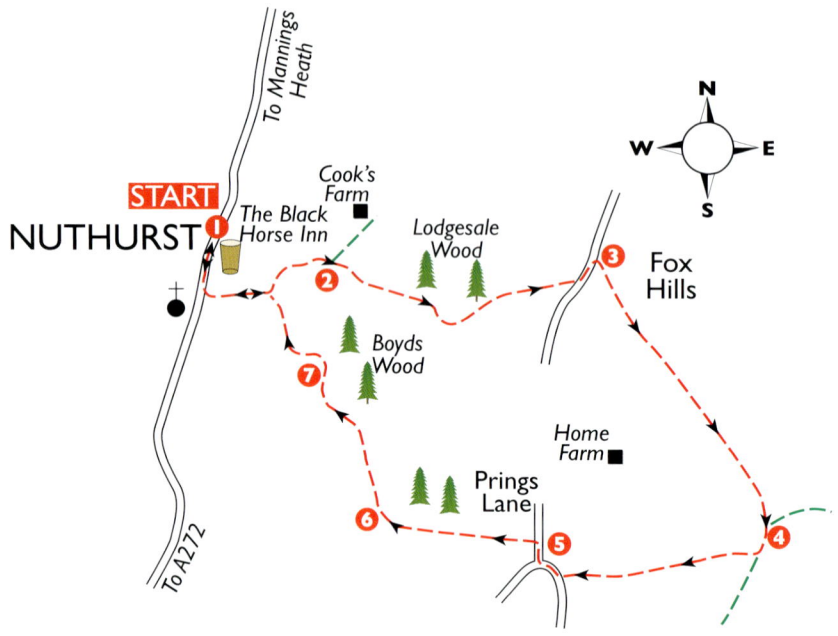

❷ In 10 metres, ignore a footpath to the left and press on ahead along the bridleway. The bridleway is easily followed through the glorious woodland and ends at a road beside a cottage after ¾ mile.

❸ Turn left along the lane and, immediately after passing the cottage, turn right on a public bridleway that again leads through woodland. Keep to the bridleway and, in ¾ mile, cross a footbridge. At a junction of bridleways, follow the one signed right and on a downward slope look out for a footpath signed rightwards.

❹ Turn right here to soon enter a field. Follow the right-hand field edge; pass a barn and a gate to meet a cart track which you should follow to its end at a lane. Turn right along the lane to meet a road junction and turn right into **Prings Lane** signed to **Horsham**.

❺ In 45 metres, turn left over a stile and enter a field. Go ahead and follow a grassy path with a line of poplar trees close to your

Nuthurst

left. At the field end, pass through a ribbon of woodland and continue along the left side of the next field and cross a stile at its end and go right to a second stile.

6 Turn right along the field edge and, before its end, fork left to a marker post in the top left corner. Cross a stile, enter woodland and keep to the well-trodden path between trees to meet a T-junction at the edge of the woodland. Turn right on the well-trodden path that ends at a gate.

7 Go left through the gate and cross the field to a directional post at the far side. Turn right along the field edge and at its end press on ahead to rejoin the drive to **Cook's Farm**. Now turn left and retrace your steps back to the pub and the end of this circuit.

Place of Interest Nearby

Bolney Wine Estate is one of the longest established English vineyards and is open to the public. Learn about the award-winning English wines and the craft behind them. Just drop in or join one of the guided tours with tastings. There is a café, shop and restaurant offering home-cooked dishes with of course the estate wines. The vineyard is 7 miles south-east of Nuthurst and is open each day from 9am until 5pm (Friday closing 10.30pm). Foxhole Lane, Bolney. **Sat Nav:** RH17 5NB.
⊕ bolneywineestate.com ☎ 01444 881575

Walk 18

HENFIELD

Distance: 4¼ miles (6.8 km)

Map: OS Explorer OL11 Brighton & Hove **Grid Ref:** TQ206162

How to get there: Henfield sits astride the A281, 4½ miles south of Cowfold and 4 miles west of Hurstpierpoint. From the northern end of the High Street opposite The White Hart Inn turn into Church Road then continue along Upper Station Road to reach The Cat & Canary pub. **Sat Nav:** BN5 9PJ.

Parking: At The Cat & Canary, with permission; the small car park beside it or alongside Station Road.

This easy, level circuit leaves the pub by following the Downs Link long-distance path that passes its door. The path is 37 miles long in total and links the North Downs Way to the South Downs Way National Trails; this section utilises the track bed of British Rail's Steyning Line that was closed in 1966 during the infamous

Henfield 18

Beeching Cuts. The route offers almost 2 miles of walking along what has become an unofficial linear nature reserve and a pleasure to explore. When the path meets with the River Adur, the way turns and continues alongside the scenic water's edge as it passes through meadows with lovely views. Turning once again, the route follows a pleasant bridleway along farm tracks and drives as it makes its return to the pub.

THE PUB **THE OLD RAILWAY** is ideally situated right next to the Downs Link long-distance path that is enjoyed by cyclists and walkers alike. Much has changed since the pub was built in Victorian times to serve the commuters who used the newly built railway station. Then it was called the Station Hotel, later becoming the Cat and Canary and in more recent years called the Old Railway Tavern. The railway station and commuters have long gone and have been replaced by walkers and cyclists who enjoy the long-distance path. The pub serves a good selection of ales and food and has a good-sized welcoming garden is set out with tables during summer.

⊕ theoldrailwayhenfield.co.uk ☎ 01273 492509

The Walk

❶ With your back to **The Old Railway**, cross the road and continue ahead down **Station Road** soon passing the ironically named '**Beechings**' modern housing development built on the site of the old railway station. At the foot of the slope, when the road bends sharply left, turn right to meet the signed **Downs Link path** in 30 metres.

❷ Turn left along the Downs Link path that utilises the old track bed and ignore all side paths. Remain on this lovely path where later you may get a chance of spotting a deer or two grazing on

West Sussex Pub Walks

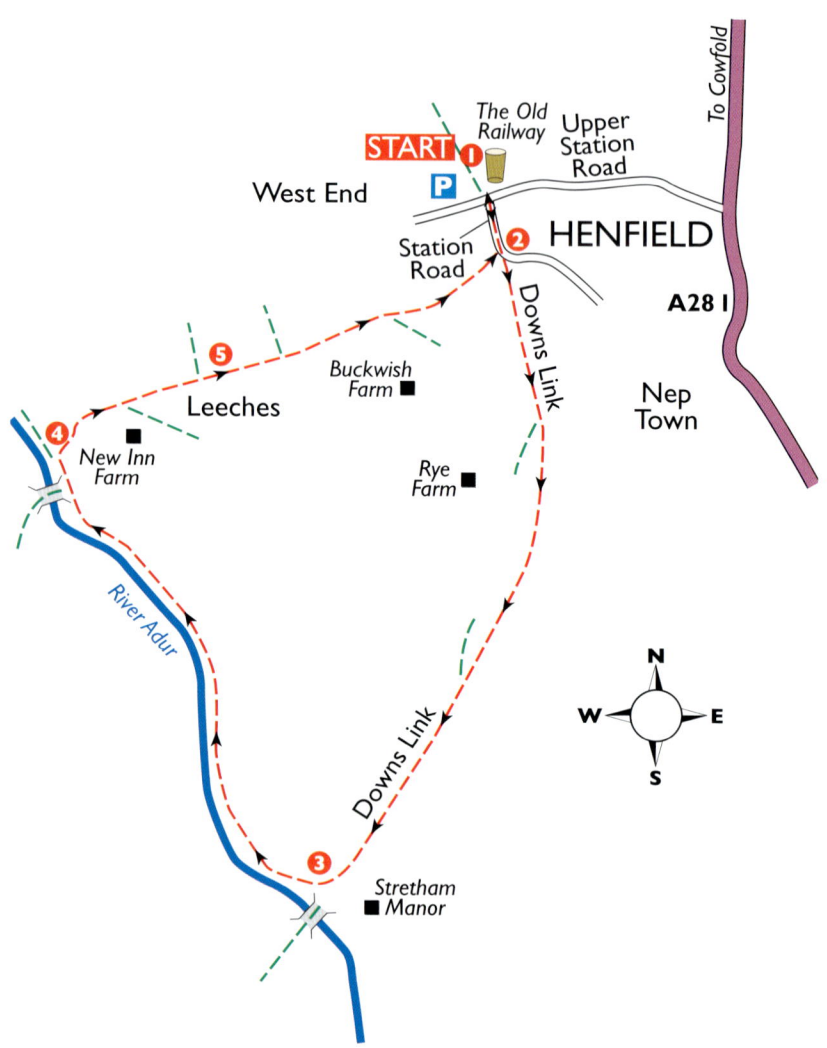

the hedgerows that line the way. After almost 2 miles, a metal bridge over the **River Adur** will be seen ahead of you.

❸ Cross a stile on your right 20 metres before the bridge is met and now follow the riverside path through several meadows for 1½ miles where the views to the South Downs are far-reaching.

Henfield

4 Finally, a bridge over the river is met. Cross a stile ahead of you and go ahead on a well-used bridleway that soon turns its back on the river and passes by the buildings of **New Inn Farm**.

5 Keep ahead on this well-signed bridleway as it continues along farm drives, cart tracks and a lane to finally rejoin the **Downs Link path**. Go ahead here and in 30 metres turn left into **Station Road** where **The Old Railway** will be met at its end.

Place of Interest Nearby

Henfield Museum is in Coopers Way just off the High Street and has exhibits ranging from fossils to household items through the ages that reflect past times in the town. There is a penny-farthing from 1887, a one-man ambulance used until the 1930s and relics from the railway that once served the town.
⊕ henfieldhub.com/henfield-museum ☎ 01273 492507

Walk 19
PYECOMBE

Distance: 6½ miles (10.4 km)

Map: OS Explorer OL11 Brighton & Hove **Grid Ref:** TQ291124

How to get there: Pyecombe is 7 miles north of Brighton at the junction of the A23 and A273. When travelling north from Brighton follow the inside lane signed to A273 Hassocks and similarly when travelling south follow the signs to A273 Hassocks. Both routes are then signed to the pub and Pyecombe Services. **Sat Nav:** BN45 7FN.

Parking: At The Plough pub with permission, or in the long layby to its left.

This good, invigorating walk over the South Downs begins in Pyecombe, a village most people miss as they speed to and

… from Brighton on the busy A23 dual carriageway. The village is ancient and the name Pyecombe is thought to date back to Saxon times. The route follows the South Downs Way long-distance path out of the village and slowly gains height to reach the top of the Downs and far-reaching views over the surrounding countryside. The route is undulating, well signed and easy to follow. When Ditchling Beacon is reached, the route turns southward and begins to lose height as it passes through the peace and tranquillity of North Bottom to meet Lower Standean. Heading back from here the way offers further magnificent views before it returns to the village.

THE PLOUGH is open all day and is ideally situated close to the South Downs Way long-distance path which is excellent news for the many walkers who pass through Pyecombe village. The comfortable bar is well-stocked and a wide range of food is on offer whether from the simple bar menu with choices that include filled baguettes and ploughman's platters to a much wider selection from the extensive and Italian-influenced main menu. After the walk, why not relax at a table in the comfortable bar, the conservatory or under a colourful umbrella at a table in the sunny garden where there are good views across the South Downs?

⊕ theploughpyecombe.co.uk   ☎ 01273 842796

The Walk

❶ Walk up **Church Lane** beside the pub to meet a T-junction and turn right along **School Lane** to reach the A273 road. Turn left on a path parallel with the road that ends at the busy main road with the driveway of **Pyecombe Golf Club** opposite. With caution, cross to the driveway and continue on the signed **South Downs Way** that passes the car park and clubhouse.

❷ Press on ahead along a well-signed driveway that later becomes a stony cart track and at the top of the hill passes a picnic table and seats. At a junction of tracks, leave the South Downs Way by continuing ahead on a path that later passes through a gate, turns left and ends at a T-junction where it rejoins the South Downs Way.

West Sussex Pub Walks

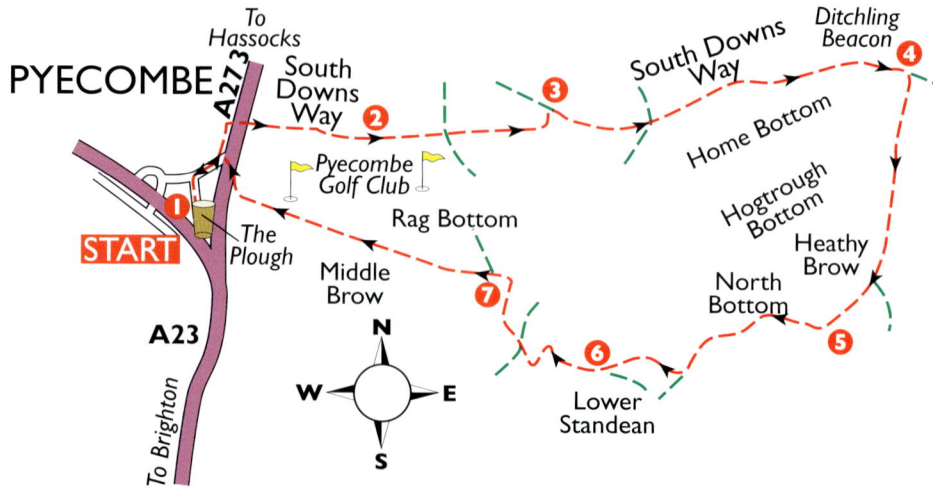

❸ Turn right here along the path across the top of the Downs. At the top of a rise, ignore a bridleway signed right to the **Chattri Memorial** and another signed left to **Hassocks**. Keep ahead to meet **Ditchling Beacon** in 1 mile where the next bridleway is signed to the right.

Ditchling Beacon at 814 ft (248m) above sea level is one of the highest points on the South Downs and as the name suggests, it was one of a chain of beacons lit to warn of impending invasion.

❹ Turn right on this bridleway that offers views over Brighton and the sea. At the bottom of a slope, pass through a gate and ignore a footpath off to the left. The route forks right on a grassy path that continues downhill along the valley floor.

❺ At the foot of the slope the path passes trees and goes through a gate before continuing along the valley floor. Eventually, pass through a pedestrian gate and maintain direction. As the track soon bends left, fork right on a rising cart track that ends at a T-junction beside a farmyard at **Lower Standean**.

Pyecombe 19

6 Turn right and now follow a chalky track that goes uphill between fields. After passing a brick barn the track turns left alongside a field edge. At the top of the rise when the track turns sharp left into a field, continue ahead on the signed bridleway to meet a gate. Follow the path right here and, at the next gate, follow it left.

7 Now go ahead over the open Downs and ignore a bridleway to the right. The path is straight and crosses **Pyecombe Golf Course** twice where you should look out for flying golf balls. After losing height alongside a field, the bridleway finally bends right and ends back at the A273. With caution, cross the road diagonally right to rejoin **School Lane** and retrace your steps back to the pub.

West Sussex Pub Walks

Place of Interest Nearby

Ditchling Museum of Art + Craft is 3½ miles north-west of Pyecombe. It hosts a permanent collection of artists' work as well as a changing programme of exhibitions. There is also a shop and café housed in a converted Grade II-listed cart shed. Lodge Hill Lane (off the B2116), Ditchling. **Sat Nav:** BN6 8SP. ⊕ ditchlingmuseumartcraft.org.uk ☎ 01273 844744

Ardingly Reservoir

Walk 20
BALCOMBE

Distance: 7¼ miles (11.6 km)

Map: OS Explorer 135 Ashdown Forest **Grid Ref:** TQ309306

How to get there: Balcombe is 4 miles (6.4 km) south-east of junction 10a of the M23. Go south along the B2036 and just before entering the village, turn left at a mini-roundabout into Haywards Heath Road signed to Borde Hill Garden to meet The Half Moon Inn. **Sat Nav:** RH17 6PA.

Parking: Limited at the pub, so park considerately around the village.

Moments after leaving Balcombe the route immerses itself in the tranquil charm of the countryside as it crosses fields and along a quiet lane on its way to the waters of Ardingly Reservoir. The scenery here is stunning and is complemented by the colourful sailboats that weave back and forth on the shimmering water

West Sussex Pub Walks

as their crews work the light breeze. The scenic path follows the water's edge for two miles to reach the southern bank where the route leaves the reservoir and joins with the Ouse Valley Way long-distance path. Following this path, the way passes through pretty fields before going under the Ouse Valley Viaduct, a striking feature in the countryside here. Pressing on through more lovely scenery, the route heads west before turning back to rejoin Balcombe.

THE PUB

THE HALF MOON INN is at the centre of village life in Balcombe, so much so that when the owners, a large pub chain, wanted to close it down, 300 villagers banded together and raised the money to buy it and turn it into a community-owned pub. Thankfully they were successful and the pub

exudes plenty of country charm and offers a selection of well-kept cask beers and a good variety of home-cooked food that will please all. The pub is popular and due to its small size it is always best to book a table if wishing to eat here. Dogs are welcome and dog biscuits are often available so your four-legged friend will not feel left out.

⊕ facebook.com/halfmoonbalcombe   ☎ 01444 811582

The Walk

❶ With your back to the pub, go left and follow the road right that soon passes between fields to reach **Balcombe's cricket field**. Go left around the boundary then continue on a path through trees to a kissing gate. Ignore a path ahead and turn right down the field edge, cross a bridge and go half left over the next field to a stile and a lane.

❷ Turn left along the lane and follow it right at a bend. In 50 metres, turn right on a bridleway through woodland. At the end of the woodland pass through a gate, turn left and go left through a second gate and continue through woodland via steps to rejoin the road. Go ahead along the road passing the old mill that now

Balcombe 20

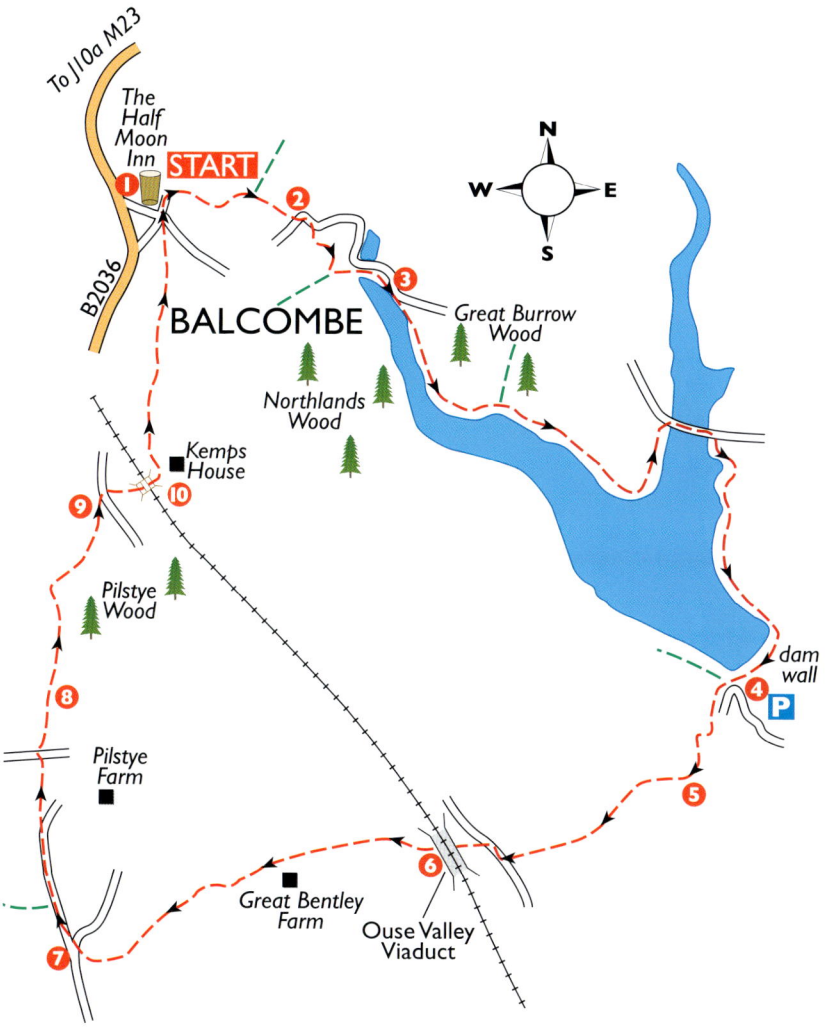

serves as a residence and press on up the road to meet a gate on your right.

❸ Pass through the gate and follow a path along the water's edge for 1¾ miles. The path ends at a gate with a road beyond. Turn right alongside the road to meet a gate on your right. Go right

West Sussex Pub Walks

here and follow the waterside path to meet the reservoir dam in 1,200 metres.

❹ Continue to the end of the dam, cross a tarmac area. Ahead of you is a tarmac drive and two narrow paths to its right; choose the path dead ahead and ignore the one forking right. Go ahead, pass through a kissing gate and follow the left field edge and around to the right to enter a second field. Press on along the left edge and cross a bridge at its end.

❺ Go ahead, cross a second bridge and ignore a path ahead. Fork right and pass through a couple of fields to meet a road. Turn right along the road and, soon after passing a cottage, turn left over a stile. Follow the path across a field passing under the **Ouse Valley Viaduct** to meet a farm track. Turn left and then right between **Ryelands Farmhouse** and barns.

The viaduct was completed in 1842 and stands 30 metres high and 460 metres long. It took 11 million bricks to build the 37 arches. The Grade II-listed viaduct still carries more than 100 trains each day.

❻ In 25 metres, fork left at a footpath sign and follow the field edge to meet and cross two stiles in quick succession. Cross a field diagonally half left to its distant corner. Cross a stile and press on to meet and cross a footbridge. Press on ahead to finally go up steps to join the driveway of **Great Bentley Farm**. Go ahead along the drive that ends at a road.

❼ Cross the road diagonally left and turn right into **Cherry Lane**. Continue along this lane ignoring a footpath to the left. At a bend where the road crosses a stream, fork left on a signed path. Follow the left field edge and pass through a hedgerow at its end to meet a lane. Turn left for 30 metres before turning right on the signed path which you should follow towards an oak tree at the top of the rise.

❽ Pass the tree; go through a gate, cross a small meadow and over a stile before pressing on ahead along the left side of a field. The path enters woodland and passes sandstone cliffs to meet a broad crossing track. Go ahead on a narrow path to a

Balcombe 20

directional post before bearing right downhill between trees to meet a kissing gate.

9 Enter a field where the sign indicates the path goes through its centre. If a crop is growing, follow the left field edge. Both ways lead to a stile in its corner where you should follow a narrow path to meet a road. Go left alongside the road before soon crossing to a drive opposite. Pass barns; go through the gates of a large house to meet a directional post to the right of the short drive.

10 Pass through a gate and follow the path; cross a railway footbridge and continue on the path to meet a field. Press on along the right side the field and, at its end, go ahead and seek out a narrow path forking left to pass between houses and meet a road. Cross the road to one opposite and when this bends left, go ahead on an enclosed path. Pass the side of a recreation ground and press on to meet a village street and go ahead to rejoin **The Half Moon Inn**.

Place of Interest Nearby

Borde Hill Garden is 2½ miles south of Balcombe. There are 200 acres of park, woodland and gardens to explore and it is most famous for its rare shrubs and trees that were collected by Victorian plant collectors. Since then, four generations of the Clarke family have lovingly tended the gardens and opened them to the public. Borde Hill Lane, Haywards Heath. **Sat Nav:** RH16 1XP.   ⊕ bordehill.co.uk   ☎ 01444 450326

Ouse Valley Viaduct

OTHER TITLES FROM COUNTRYSIDE BOOKS

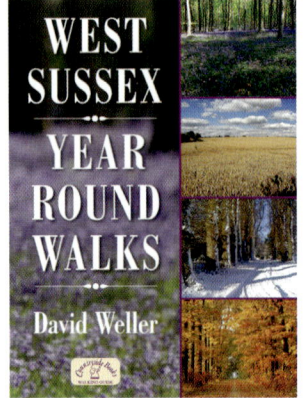
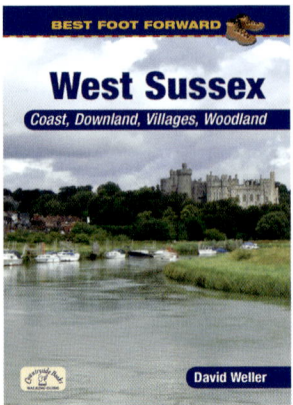

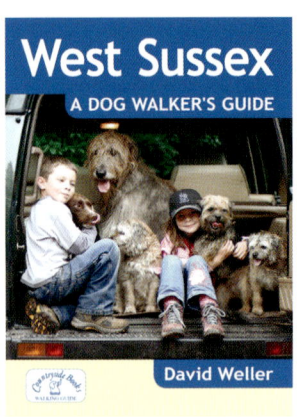

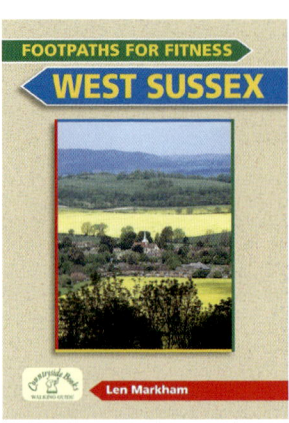
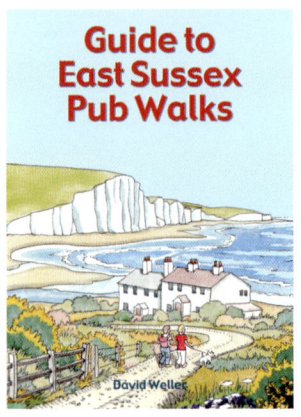
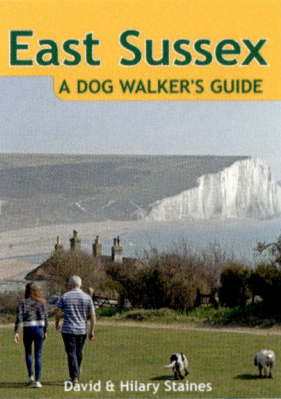
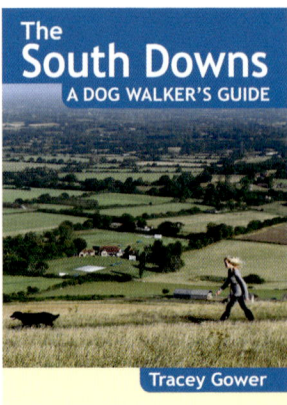

To see the full range of books by Countryside Books please visit
www.countrysidebooks.co.uk
Follow us on  @CountrysideBooks